AN HONOUR AND A PRIVILEGE

Whatever sport you play, wearing the colours of your country is the ultimate privilege.

I feel lucky to have done that 79 times over the course of more than a decade and I cherish so many good memories from that time.

I hope there's a little way to go for me at the highest level yet, and the World Cup later this year could turn out to be a fairly important chapter of my career.

But whatever happens out in New Zealand in the autumn, I feel blessed to have done what I have.

I'm just an ordinary lad from the Amman Valley who has been able to fulfill his dream with the help of family, friends and plenty of great players along the way.

I want to thank everyone who has ever followed my progress down the years – I've had some wonderful support from people through good times and bad.

And I hope you enjoy flicking through this souvenir magazine as much as I have enjoyed helping to put it all together.

All the best,

CONTENTS

14

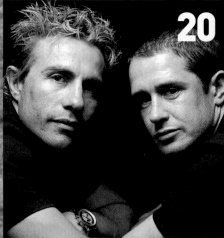

20

36

56

Content: Delme Parfitt

Design & Production:
Alan Jewell, James Kenyon

Executive Editor: Ken Rogers
Senior Editor: Steve Hanrahan
Senior Art Editor: Rick Cooke
Senior Production Editor: Paul Dove

Photographic credits:
Huw Evans Picture Agency
Trinity Mirror

© Published in Great Britain in 2011 by
Trinity Mirror Sport Media, PO Box 48, Old Hall Street,
Liverpool L69 3EB.

Taking on the Australia
defence in November 2010

THE PRINCE OF WALES

Delme Parfitt, rugby writer for Media Wales and the man who helped compile Shane's autobiography, provides a personal insight into the winger who has thrilled the nation for over a decade by tearing opposition defences apart

Everyone loves Shane. He's just cool, easy-going, down-to-earth. There's nothing complicated about him. He just goes out on the field, has a go, invariably plays bloody well and ends up winning you games on so many occasions. We hate being without him.

That was the gist of the assessment from former Wales and Lions captain Gareth Thomas when I asked him, not long before he retired from the international game, to sum up the contribution of Shane Mark Williams.

It's the final sentence that has the greatest resonance for me now. Before long, Welsh rugby won't have Shane to call on anymore. At 34 years of age he is in the late autumn of his career even if he shows no physical signs of waning just yet. It may not be until he is gone that we fully appreciate what we had.

When a fresh-faced choirboy was called into the Wales side by Graham Henry for a Six Nations clash with France in 2000 there were those who scoffed. One or two heavy tackles, said the doubters, and this little whipper-snapper from the Amman Valley would never be seen again.

Fast-forward 11 years and Shane has become one of the legends of the modern game.

There's the 79 caps for his country, the record number of tries, the two Lions tours, the two World Cups, the countless pieces of magic that have got every team he has represented out of a tight corner at some stage.

And all this from a fellow who was supposed to be too small to cut it among the highest company.

Perhaps he was too small in those early days, but his triumph was always his ability to adapt.

SHANE TRIBUTES

"No one plays quite like Williams. What he does and how he does it cannot be written down. To attempt to explain what he does can go only half the way. To know what he does, he must be seen. It is the synchronisation of the several actions, of the rhythm and the tempo of the whole deed, that accomplishes the "magic" of the deception; and of the infinite variety. There is no quiet end of the day when Williams is prowling mischievously around. He is a free spirit. There are times when he fails, trying to do too much. That's his nature."

Gerald Davies, former Wales winger and manager of the 2009 Lions tour to South Africa

"As a player, I was fortunate to play alongside the likes of J J Williams, Viv Jenkins and Gerald Davies, to name but three. For me, they were three of the greatest exponents of wing play our national game has ever seen. There have been others since then – Ieuan Evans immediately springs to mind as a player of great quality and one who people in Wales, and further afield for that matter, would queue up to watch.
As far as I'm concerned, Shane Williams is up there with the aforementioned players, not only as a try scorer, but as a genuine entertainer. His sidestep at pace reminds me of the great Gerald Davies while his ability to overcome his size (or lack of it) makes a mockery of those who have constantly criticised him for being, simply, too small."

JPR Williams, former Wales full-back

Looks are deceiving nowadays. As strong as an Ox and blessed with the physical attributes of a world-class gymnast, Shane is these days as durable and fearless on the rugby field as any of his peers.

He retains lightning pace off the mark, silky ball skills and the kind of innate sense of timing and opportunity possessed of all the greatest wingers.

No wonder in 2008, the greatest year of his career, he entered the realms of rugby immortality by becoming the only Welshman ever to win the prestigious International Rugby Board Player of the Year award.

Considering how decorated Shane is, it would be no surprise to many if he were aloof, unapproachable and remote from the ordinary people who flock to watch him week in, week out. But it's quite the opposite. Thomas was spot on in the assessment alluded to above, perhaps because of the upbringing which forced him to work for everything he ever had.

'He is as strong as an Ox and blessed with the physical attributes of a world-class gymnast'

"It helps any team if they have players with the X-factor. We are fortunate to have two or three in the side and Shane is definitely one of those. Shane is a very talented player. You need players who can create something out of nothing."

Warren Gatland, Wales head coach

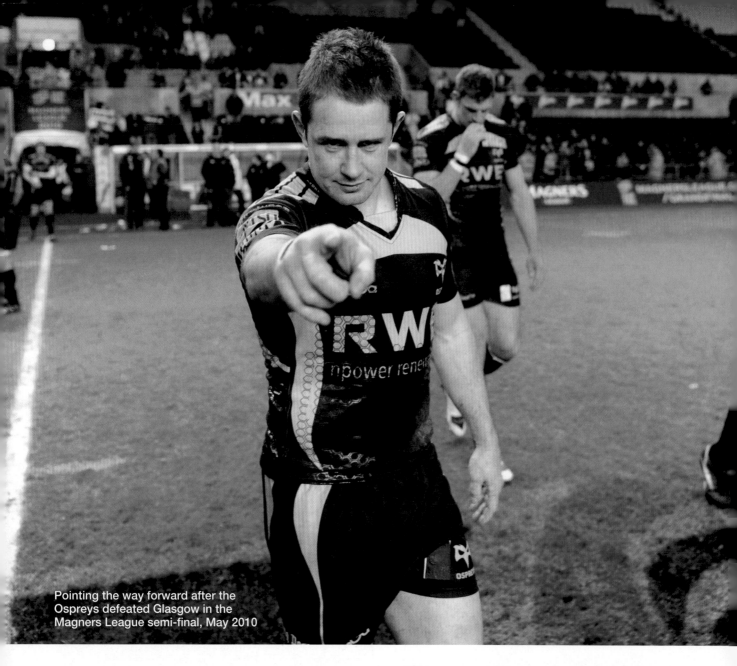

Pointing the way forward after the
Ospreys defeated Glasgow in the
Magners League semi-final, May 2010

He's worked in factories, at a bakery, for the employment service and a double-glazing firm.

When he got his first rugby opportunity with Neath he used to paint the stands after training and drive around in a battered old Ford Fiesta.

He went through the pain of his parents divorcing as a young boy, but his mother and grandparents kept him grounded, gave him a loving childhood which saw him get into the usual scrapes, whether it was scarpering from irate neighbours during games of 'Jonny Knockin' or getting ten bells knocked out of him protecting his younger brother Dean in some playground dispute.

He had the same hopes and dreams as other boys, and suffered the same heartache, like dealing with the sudden loss of his beloved pet golden retriever, Buckley.

"All I can remember is sitting on the settee at my gran's house crying my eyes out," he recalled.

Manifold other experiences will have shaped his personality. They combined to good effect.

In all the years I have worked with Shane, it is his level-headedness and polite and affable nature that has impressed me most.

Never once have I seen him be rude or confrontational to a team-mate or a member of the media corps and in dark times for the Wales team, such as the awful 2007 World Cup exit at the hands of Fiji, he has so often been

'He used to paint the stands after training and drive around in a battered old Ford Fiesta'

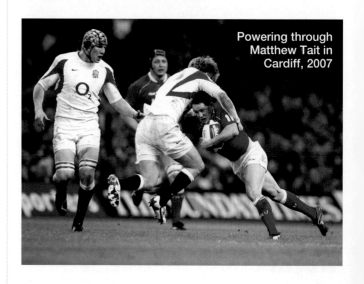

Powering through
Matthew Tait in
Cardiff, 2007

England captain Mike Tindall is left sprawling in the opening game of the 2011 Six Nations

the first to face the music, fronting up to cameras and microphones while others slunk away.

I worked with him on his autobiography in 2008, the year when his star was rocketing into orbit because of his exploits as part of Warren Gatland's Grand Slam-winning side.

We would meet in cafes and pubs to get his life recorded on tape and so many people couldn't resist approaching him, be it for his signature, a photograph or just to say hello.

The reaction was always the same, a cheery greeting, a friendly word and an obliging nature no matter what the request.

And throughout all our dealings, Shane has always struck me as a fellow who will never lose sight of his priorities.

It said it all that he talked about his family life and his childhood with as much - if not more – enthusiasm as his achievements on the field.

Taking care of his family, wife Gail, daughter Georgie and son Carter, as well as brother Dean, sisters Hayley and Beth, mam Christine and dad Mark is what matters most to Shane, and always will.

Christine used to scrimp and save to buy her eldest son a pair of boots, at one time taking on two jobs to see to it that she could.

And you can see the pride come alive in Shane's eyes when he tells of instances like that.

You sense he remains eternally grateful for the gift of being one of the greatest rugby players in the world, because if coaches like Lyn Jones, then of Neath, and Henry, had not placed their faith in him, he so easily may have slipped under the radar and never made it at all.

He knows the greatest adventure of his life is about to come to an end and he wants it to conclude on a high.

What better way for him to do it than as part of a successful Wales team at the World Cup later this year?

If Shane can light up the bid of Gatland's boys in New Zealand, he may even go on a bit longer than anticipated.

Few would complain. We need to make the most of Shane Williams while we still can.

Because, more's the pity, he won't be around forever.

SHANE TRIBUTES

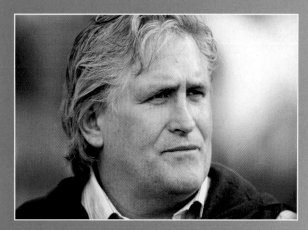

"He's unbelievable, he just defies all logic. It's a privilege to have known the kid. He's just one out of the bag that you can't explain."

Scott Johnson, Ospreys head coach

"What a player! He's the sort of guy you are just glad is on your side and not among the opposition."

Shaun Edwards, Wales defence coach and Wasps head coach

"Shane is an exciting player who really lives every moment of a game and gets really pumped up. It comes with the territory and is part of the game. I have a lot of respect for him – Shane is one of the most respected players in the world."

Bryan Habana, South Africa winger and 2007 IRB Player of the Year

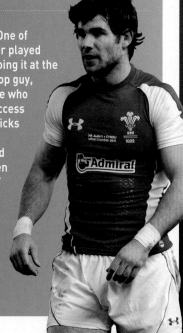

"Shane is a living legend. One of the best players I have ever played alongside and he's been doing it at the top for years. He's also a top guy, a great friend and someone who has never let any of his success go to his head. I hope he sticks around as long as possible playing for the Ospreys and Wales. We'll miss him when he's not with us anymore."

Mike Phillips, Ospreys and Wales scrum-half

Offloading as Mike Catt prepares to tackle him on his third Wales appearance in 2000

GROWING UP AND MAKING IT BIG

A self-confessed "tearaway" as a youngster, Shane had an opportunity to develop a football career but rugby was always his first love

You may like to know where I learned to side-step. Well, it could well have been dodging my way around bar stools in the Cross Keys pub in Glanamman, which my mam and dad used to keep.

That's my earliest memory of a home life, in that pub, and I remember the old faces who used to drink there and the smell that you only used to get in pubs in the day when smoking inside was still allowed.

I was a bit of a tearaway as a youngster, I couldn't sit still for two minutes and that is what my little daughter Georgie is like these days.

The Cross Keys was only a small place and our living quarters were tiny. We ended up moving from there when my younger brother Dean came along and we went off to a two-bedroom council house nearby.

I never saw much of my dad, Mark, who was always away driving lorries in Europe and I did miss him badly.

Mam and dad divorced in 1986, which I found quite upsetting because I thought it would just mean that I saw dad much less.

In the event, I did. I idolised him. He was a local character who was renowned for working hard and playing hard and there were times when I would yearn to see him.

But mam kept the family going, ensuring that me and Dean never wanted for any of life's essentials by doing two jobs at times, although things like school trips and foreign holidays were never even on the radar.

And my grandparents, Mary and Emrys, who I love dearly, also lived nearby and I was forever paying them visits.

I was quite a tough little kid in many ways, I had to

Looking like a boy in a man's world, he is lifted aloft by Wales prop Peter Rogers after scoring two tries against Scotland in March 2000, shortly after his 23rd birthday

look out for Dean and got myself into no end of scrapes defending him at times, and I also tended to play in teams with older boys, for example playing in an under-14 team when I was just 11. Maybe that is where I learned to take the knocks that I do now, I was forever taking hefty challenges but I always got up and I have maintained that right through to the present day.

Me and Dean had what you might term a turbulent relationship at times, getting into the sorts of fights brothers always do.

We had a scrap once at a barbecue because I wouldn't let him do the cooking and after I locked him in the kitchen he slid a skewer underneath the door trying to still get at me in some way!

Down the years we've had our fair share of toe-to-toes. We've even gone outside of pubs on occasion to sort out disagreements with our fists. After trying to knock lumps out of one another we'd come round with a few conciliatory words and it would always be resolved with no grudges ever borne.

I have always been frightened to hurt him because of the naturally protective instincts I have as an elder brother, but the truth is these days he is far bigger than me anyway!

I do have a different relationship with my sister Hayley,

you may not be surprised to learn. She is great with people, everyone loves her and we barely ever have a cross word.

At school my favourite pastime wasn't rugby at all, but gymnastics. I liked the danger of it, the risk that unless you executed a move properly you could come a cropper. I was hooked to the point where I'd spend almost every lunch-hour in the gym.

But I also loved football and played for Cwmamman United juniors and then Cwmamman in the Neath league.

Alan Curtis came to watch me once and said there might be the prospect of trials with Swansea City, but when I was in my late teens I knew that Neath Rugby Club were interested in me and when Lyn Jones telephoned me out of the blue one day, I was only ever going to choose one path.

When that approach came I was almost on my way to Blaydon, a club affiliated to Aviva Premiership club Newcastle.

They had offered me the chance to play for them after someone had spotted me playing for Amman United and my bags were as good as packed before Lyn rang.

But I've always been a home bird and the chance to play for my local club was one I was never going to turn down.

There was no promise of a long contract but after training with them for the summer they started paying me about

Alan Curtis offered him a trial at Swansea City

Dale McIntosh was an intimidating opponent

Lyn Jones

'Lyn Jones was a huge influence on me, even though his methods and personality were unconventional'

£130 a week and threw in a car too, even if it was a heap of junk that looked like it had been driven down an alley too narrow for it.

I had to wait a while for a proper chance with Neath, but when I finally got to play a first team match it could not have been a tougher one, away to Pontypridd who at the time were a real force in Welsh rugby in a match that was live on TV.

I remember getting smashed in one tackle by their giant back row talisman Dale McIntosh and I wondered if would ever be able to cut it physically in the game.

But I just had to steel myself by realising that if I ducked out now I would never make it back.

I guess my decision to stick with it was borne out when we went to Perpignan for a Heineken Cup tie.

We lost by 40-odd points but I had a good game, making a few second half breaks that really caught the eye. I played a bit at scrum-half back then, but every time I went to the wing I loved the freedom of it all and especially the fact that I didn't have to worry about my fingers getting trodden on at rucks!

Anyway, after the match the Perpignan chairman wanted to sign me on the spot, offering Neath a fee of £15,000. It didn't happen of course, but it was a good bargaining tool. Neath decided to give me a proper one-year contract and for the first time I felt like a professional player.

Those early days were a lot madder than things are now. We were still adjusting to professionalism and some of the drinking games on away trips nearly proved my undoing.

But I gradually began to make my mark.

Lyn Jones was a huge influence on me, even though his methods and personality were unconventional.

Lyn is a bit of a maverick in the game, but most of what he got us to do worked, he was very brave and innovative in what he did and perhaps that rubbed off on me as I went through my career.

MY PHOTO ALBUM

Part 1

Shane tells us the story behind the pictures from some memorable moments during his career, on and off the pitch

My first appearance against England, aged 23, at Twickenham

England, March 2000

My first visit to Twickenham was not a happy one. We lost 46-12, it was the hardest match I had ever played in physically and I'd had Austin Healey chopsing in my ear all game. To top it all off, Ben Cohen, pictured here on the left, apparently said "Shane Who?" when asked about me afterwards. It caused a media storm and Ben even felt he had to apologise to me. But I didn't care about all the fuss half as much as others did.

Try v Scotland, March 2000

Crossing for a try against Scotland in what would have been my second ever for Wales.
   You can see on my face what it meant. I have always loved scoring tries for Wales but back in 2000 it was still a real novelty. At this stage I still didn't know if I was going to cut it as a Test player, so every score was a huge boost to my confidence.

Thrilled to be scoring for my country in Cardiff

Running at Joe Worsley and Julian White during the opening match of the 2005 Six Nations

⌃ England win, February 2005

Happier times against the old enemy saw us beat them in the first match of our Grand Slam campaign of 2005. Looks like I'm cruising for a bruising here though, trying to squeeze between two man-mountains in Julian White and Joe Worsley.

⊳ Fashion shoot, February 2005

A shot that causes me embarrassment to be honest. It's a promotional thing for Eden Park clothing with me, Gareth Thomas, Gavin Henson and Stephen Jones strutting our stuff down St Mary's Street in the centre of Cardiff. Can't remember what flavour the lollipop was!

Turning heads in Cardiff, 2005

Parading the Six Nations trophy in front of a delirious crowd at the Millennium Stadium after the Grand Slam had been secured against Ireland, March 2005

Parading Six Nations trophy, March 2005

This was the first thing I'd ever won with Wales – the 2005 Grand Slam – and here we are walking around the pitch in triumph after beating Ireland. The only problem was I overdid it on the celebrating afterwards. We went to a few pubs in Cardiff and the next morning I had the mother and father of all hangovers!

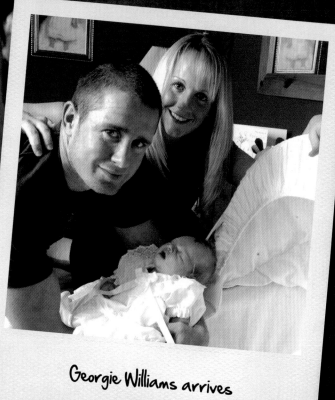

Georgie Williams arrives

Holding the baby, 2006

This is me and my wife Gail with our first child Georgie not long after she arrived.

Having kids changes your life and it's strange to look at her here when I think of the bundle of energy she is now.

'I've had a few incidents with bikes in my time – I fell off one once and seriously hurt my elbow – but this was good safe fun'

›› Quad biking, October 2007

This was at a track in Ty Croes near where I live in the Amman Valley. I was doing a publicity shot for a magazine and welcomed the chance to have a go on the quad bikes.

I've had a few incidents with bikes in my time – I fell off one once and seriously hurt my elbow – but this was good safe fun.

Fast on four wheels and two legs

A close call...but the try was given

⌃ Try v Scotland, February 2008

A controversial try in our 30-15 win against Scotland in 2008. I made a break from quite a way out and arced my way towards the corner. My Ospreys team-mate Nikki Walker got across to make a last-ditch tackle but by the time he arrived I was in mid-air diving for the line. Thankfully it went to the video ref and was ruled good. Was my foot in touch? Did I touch the corner flag? To this day I couldn't tell you. But what I do is that the try stood...all that matters really!

Holding still while the artist is at work

▲ Portrait, 2008

Me posing for a portrait for artist Andrew Vicari. I didn't know much about him but after doing some research it appealed to me. It was a surreal experience though – I found it hard to sit still. We did three sittings of about two hours each in his sister's house in Neath. To me a picture is a picture. Andrew was happy with it and I have it in my house at the moment. There were three sketches done in the end, I was going to auction them, but decided against it.

≫ Six Nations, 2007

I pose in front of the Welsh flag at the start of the 2007 Six Nations. It wasn't a great year for us and it culminated with us bombing out of the World Cup and Gareth Jenkins losing his job.

Proud to represent Wales

Shane's photo album continues on page 70

BROTHERS IN ARMS

We go inside the dressing room as Shane tells us about the men he's played alongside for club and country, including Gareth Thomas and Gavin Henson

Since I've played for Wales we've had some really great characters in our midst and the friends I have made for life are one of the best parts of doing what I do.

Chris Wyatt, the former Llanelli second row was a prime example, he was a guy who was in the team when I first broke in back in 2000.

Chris was a real gentleman, Clunky we used to call him, and I had bags of time for him.

He was seen as one of the best second rows in the world at one time when Graham Henry was getting the best out of him, but for one reason or another he faded away.

Clunky was a bit of a loveable rogue I suppose, at least that's the perception I think a lot of the public had of him.

These days, my best friends in the Wales team are Lee Byrne, James Hook and Mike Phillips.

Hooky, in his own way, is one of the funniest guys I have ever met without really trying to be funny, if you know what I mean.

He has these little phrases and sayings that have us in stitches at times.

He has tons of confidence and has taken his fame in his stride. Hooky has been placed on a pedestal in Wales but he remains the sort of fellow who would do a favour for

anybody. He helped me no end during my testimonial year.

Mike Phillips, or Philsy as we call him, is a bit of a Jekyll and Hyde character. On the field he is one of the nastiest, most competitive guys you could wish to find. He's big and powerful and goes in for plenty of verbals.

I played against him a lot when he was at the Scarlets and the Blues and the number of times he has had me in a headlock is nobody's business!

One match against the Blues when Mike was with them was the day before I was due to be married.

He rubbed my face in the dirt after one tackle and said: "Put that in your wedding photos!"

When he's not playing though, Mike is a gentleman, really down to earth, even if there's a bit of a mad streak in him.

He's one of the most passionate players I've ever played with, but you need that in a team.

Tom Shanklin and Gareth Thomas have also been huge, larger than life characters who have done wonders for the spirit of the group down the years.

However, there's one guy who tops them all – Andy Powell, our No.8 who now plays his rugby with Wasps.

The funny thing about him is that he doesn't try to be

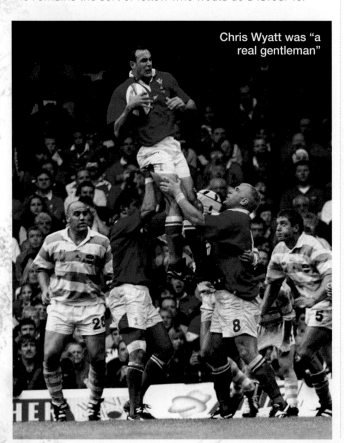

Chris Wyatt was "a real gentleman"

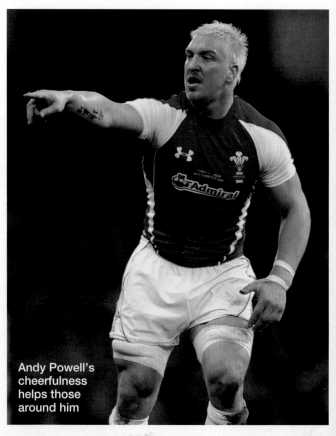

Andy Powell's cheerfulness helps those around him

'Alfie Thomas is another who lit up a room. He always had a story and was taking the mick out of someone'

funny. It's just his mannerisms and demeanour that are comical.

He has pulled a few stunts in recent times, none more well known than his little trip down the M4 in a golf buggy during the 2010 Six Nations, but he is a terrific guy who keeps us all going.

With the 2009 Lions in South Africa he really came to the fore, all the guys loved him.

Andy brightens up a room when he walks in, he is never downbeat about anything and that sort of constantly happy mood rubs off on everybody.

I've mentioned Tom Shanklin. Well, for many seasons he's been the self-appointed entertainment officer of the Wales squad.

Shanks has always taken charge of selecting the music for the team bus and the dressing room, films as well were his choice.

He's a real funny guy and clever with it as well. There's never any point trying to get one over on him, he's just too smart, especially for me.

It's a pity Shanks has had bad luck with injuries lately because he is missed so much.

Alfie Thomas is another one who, like Andy Powell, lit up a room. He always had a story, was always taking the mick out of someone and I've always said that if you want to be a professional rugby player you have to be able to accept having the mick taken out of you. If you can't then I'd advise you to do something else!

There's no hiding place at times, but I love the banter and the camaraderie that these guys engender. Without it, the squad would be the poorer.

People quite often ask me about Gavin Henson, a guy who hasn't been around us for a while now because of his time out of the game and the fact that he has since gone

'Shanks is a real funny guy and clever with it. There is never any point trying to get one over on him'

Tom Shanklin is the self-appointed entertainment officer in the Welsh squad

James Hook helped Shane during his testimonial year

Justin Marshall was a "suave city type" with his fingers in numerous pies

to Saracens and now Toulon. All I can say is that Gav is certainly different, a unique sort of person.

There seems to be a misconception among some people that he is full of himself and big-headed. Not true.

He is quiet, most of the attention he gets is unwarranted and he prefers to keep himself to himself.

After the part he played in our Grand Slam in 2005, the media interest went through the roof, fuelled by the fact his partner was Charlotte Church.

The slightest change in his hairdo seemed to spark a feeding frenzy of press attention.

Gav does pride himself on his appearance though. When he first came along his fake tan, expensive hairdos and moisturisers caused a bit of a stir because we all felt they were the sorts of things women rather than men went in for. Now, to some extent, we're all at it!

The majority of the Ospreys lads shave their legs these days, they really do, and Mike Phillips, Lee Byrne and James Hook aren't averse to the odd session on a sunbed.

Whatever, any criticism is water off a duck's back to Gav. He is one of those guys who genuinely doesn't care what people think of him.

Justin Marshall was certainly a unique bloke when he was with us at the Ospreys. A legendary New Zealand scrum-half, Justin was not short of confidence and to be honest I was a bit intimidated by him when he first joined us.

He is one of those guys who is always immaculately dressed, he'd never have a hair out of place and would breeze around in shades and expensive jackets and trousers.

His social diary was always full, he was constantly off on some golf day or heading to some glitzy dinner somewhere.

Justin was the sort who had his fingers in no end of pies, like one of those suave city types.

But he helped me enormously with my testimonial when he organised an overseas team to play against my Welsh one.

At the end of that day, all the players from both sides went to a hotel bar in Cardiff and the drinks started to flow freely.

When I went to a bar to get one in, the bartender told me Justin had put his credit card behind there and that everything was sorted.

Brilliant, I thought, and went off to join the party.

I saw him a week later at a charity function and thanked him for helping to make the day so special.

"No worries, mate," he said, before telling me to wait where I was because he'd got something for me.

He disappeared for a few minutes then returned with an envelope for me.

I opened it up to find a bill for the drinks – £1,450!

SHANE'S TOP 5 GAMES

Shane talks us through five memorable encounters when he and Wales came of age, including one that brought Grand Slam joy to the Millennium Stadium

MY BELIEF GROWS

Neath 20 Cardiff 21 (WRU National League One, September 1999)

Left: Competing for the ball with former Wales scrum-half Robert Howley during a Neath-Cardiff clash

I hadn't long been playing for Neath and I was very unsure of whether I had what it took to stay at the highest level.

But I was starting to get some good reviews and so the belief was slowly starting to build.

This was a big league game for the club against Cardiff who were always a prized scalp for us and a lot of others.

The BBC Wales cameras were at the game and so it was a great chance to make an impression.

I managed to score three tries and even though we lost, it was one of the best hat-tricks I have ever scored.

It was a great game as well, even though we didn't get the final verdict, with the lead changing hands four times.

Afterwards I couldn't believe some of the things people were saying about how well I played.

When I went home and back to the Amman United club I almost got a standing ovation!

The next day it was great to watch what I'd done on the television and have some of the pundits talk about what a prospect I was. For the first time I was enjoying some of the good press I was getting.

I began to think to myself: "Who knows, maybe I could even go on to play for Wales some day!"

Evading the New Zealand defence to create a wonderful try for Sonny Parker

HERE TO STAY

Wales 37
New Zealand 53
(World Cup Group D, November 2003)

I have spoken so many times about this game but that doesn't diminish the significance of it to my career.

Going into it there were doubts about whether I would ever be able to carry on playing international rugby, I felt like Steve Hansen had all but placed me on the scrapheap and was giving me a run out just for the sake of it.

I was determined to prove him and anyone else wrong and I felt I did that.

I just wanted to go out and enjoy it, take a few risks and see where it got me.

Fortunately it was the type of game that allowed me to do that.

When we conceded a try in the first minute and were standing underneath our own posts, plenty of people must have been rolling their eyes and thinking: "Here we go again."

But by early in the second half I was scoring a try that put us into the lead during a match that was shaping up to be the game of the tournament.

New Zealand hit back at us and went on to win; I don't think we were quite there mentally to go and secure the victory.

But that night transformed my career and marked the start of a new, more positive time for the Wales team as a whole after too many years of struggle.

It was the sort of game you fantasise about.

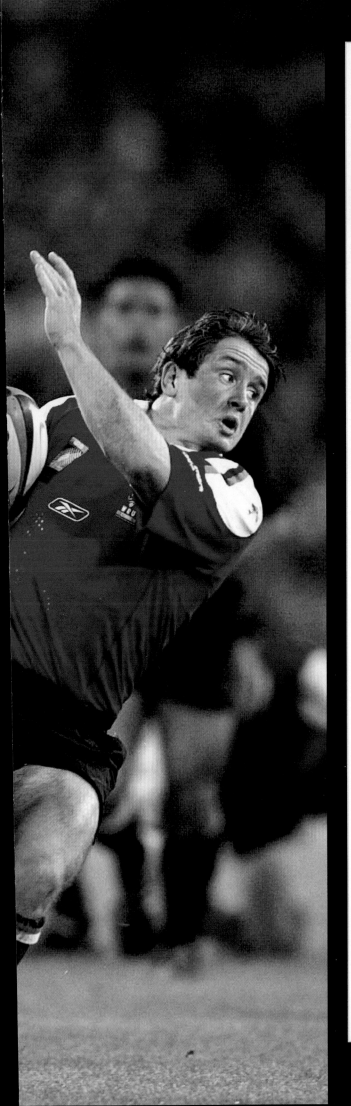

Leaving Jonny Wilkinson grasping at thin air

TURNING POINT

Wales 17 England 28 (World Cup quarter-final, November 2003)

By the time we finished this game I knew deep down that we had come through a major turning point.

England were on the glory trail that year, and their fans had followed them to Australia with enormous expectations.

Our fans are always fantastic, but the cross of St George outnumbered them heavily that evening at Brisbane's Suncorp Stadium and with Martin Johnson, Lawrence Dallaglio, Jonny Wilkinson et al to contend with on the field, we were up against it.

But the feel-good factor from the previous week's game against New Zealand had worked wonders for us and we tore into England with no fear whatsoever.

We scored two brilliantly worked tries in the first half through Stephen Jones and Colin Charvis and went in at the break leading 10-3 with England seriously rattled.

Had we been a bit more mature, a bit more used to winning games of that magnitude at the time, we could have gone on to cause a real sensation.

The English players have all since said that they knew they were in a real game that night.

But clearly a half-time rollicking from Sir Clive Woodward jolted them and they played the percentages in the second half, keeping it tight and relying on Wilkinson to kick goals.

Martyn Williams had the last word that night with a try but it was too late for us then.

All the same, it was a memorable night for me. We scared the life out of the eventual winners. The New Zealand game had been no fluke – Wales really were back.

COMEBACK KINGS

France 18 Wales 24
(Six Nations,
February 2005)

This wasn't a game that I personally lit up, but I thought I put in a good performance in what was one of the most incredible victories I have ever been involved in.

We went to Paris having beaten England and Italy, facing the real acid test of our ambitions for that year. Everyone thought it would be a task too far and when their big winger Aurelien Rougerie ran over me a few times in the first half during a French onslaught, I was beginning to think they may be right!

But the match turned immediately after half-time when Martyn Williams went over for two tries in quick succession.

Suddenly the belief started flooding through all our veins and we steadied the ship in all departments, starting to put France under serious strain.

A Stephen Jones drop goal put us in pole position but then in the final 10 minutes it was like a scene from Rorke's Drift as we defended a ferocious French assault.

Blue jerseys were raining down on us from all angles but just as it seemed the French were certain to score, a red shirt would pop up to make the tackle.

It was a heroic rearguard action and the relief when Stephen booted the ball out of play at the end of the game was massive.

It felt amazing doing our lap of honour afterwards. The win set us up to go on and win the Slam.

Side-stepping past Aurelin Rougerie

Martyn Williams dives over for his first try

Alun Wyn Jones wins a lineout under the gaze of an expectant Millennium Stadium

EYES ON THE PRIZE

Wales 29 France 12
(Six Nations, March 2008)

Everything seemed to hinge on this game, it had so many meanings.

First of all we were up for the Grand Slam against a French side who are notoriously unpredictable and secondly I needed just one more score to break Gareth Thomas's record of 40 tries for the all-time Wales record.

And it all came together in the most memorable fashion.

It was one of those days when you almost feel you can't lose, to have done so would have been too gruesome to contemplate.

We were only 9-6 ahead at the halfway mark but we were always in the ascendancy and by the time Martyn Williams fittingly got the final try, Cardiff was already bouncing to the beat of another fantastic Grand Slam party.

Shortly before Martyn had gone over, I had got my score, which came after I hacked on a loose ball and ran through to score.

I leapt what seemed like 50 feet in the air when I touched it down.

What a day!

Joy as he gets to the ball first and becomes Wales' leading try-scorer

Congratulations after his score

The two try-scorers share the Grand Slam moment

MAGIC OF THE MILLENNIUM

The greatest stadium in the world has hosted many memorable occasions in its short existence. Shane explains the magnificence of the Millennium

The Millennium Stadium is our lair, our manor, call it what you like but we don't like anyone trying to storm it. Losing there is always incredibly painful. The motto of our kit sponsors Under Armour is 'Protect this House'. That's certainly what we try to do.

It's often called the greatest stadium in the world by rugby people from all quarters, and I don't think that's an exaggeration.

How many rugby grounds these days have a 74,500 capacity and are situated slap bang in the middle of a capital city?

You just don't get that anywhere really, which is one of the reasons why it is so unique.

And it makes the bus ride to the ground on match day unique too, because you end up snaking through the crowds, through the people you know are going to be cheering you on, from the stands or from pubs in just a few hours time.

You therefore get a real sense of what it all means to them. They have all sacrificed their entire day to support you, it's what most of them have been looking forward to all week, and you do feel the responsibility to perform.

But it's when you get inside the arena that you are also struck by its uniqueness.

I've played in most of the best grounds in the world, but few give you the sense of the crowd hanging directly over the pitch like the Millennium does.

There is an intimacy about the place in the way that the stands tower steeply up around you and it makes for an electric atmosphere, especially when we are doing well.

A stage fit for heroes

Walking around the pitch after this year's victory over Ireland, potentially Shane's final Six Nations appearance in Cardiff

I swear that when Wales attack in a big match, you can physically feel the surge caused by the roar, it's an awesome experience that, to be honest, is difficult to describe.

You simply wouldn't get that at a ground where there was, say, an athletics track around the pitch.

Others simply can't offer that closeness. Twickenham, for example, is a magnificent stadium these days now that they have completed the bowl.

But for me, it's not the Millennium Stadium – though I admit I'm a bit biased!

Once we're through the crowds, the team bus goes down a ramp and turns into a little road where it stops outside the players' entrance.

The butterflies are always flying around the stomach as we get our bags and walk in, past a big silver dragon on the wall that greets you at the bottom of the stairs.

I've got my own little cubby hole in the dressing room at our ground, it's in the corner and a good spot because I can see everything that's going on from there.

I make for my own personal little spot every time we play and I wouldn't be without it.

The thrill of seeing your shirt hanging on the peg never

really goes away. Sometimes I still look at that number 11 jersey and I can't believe it's mine.

But the whole room is an environment that gives us all the creature comforts we could want.

There's drink, food, all the medical attention we could want and above all plenty of space.

There are baths galore as well, though they are usually filled with ice after games for the purposes of dealing with injuries.

You could wait around for a hot bath if you wanted – but believe me you don't want to sit in an ice one if you don't have to!

But it's being on the pitch that gives you the biggest buzz. For me, there was no better place to be in my rugby career.

Leaving the dressing room, walking out of that door and then turning the corner to walk down the tunnel and up the step onto the pitch and feeling your studs sink into the hallowed turf is a routine I will never forget.

There are just so many memories I will take from moments I have enjoyed there.

The Millennium Stadium is, for me, the greatest stadium in the world.

My other favourite stadiums
The Gnoll, Neath

The Neath squad of 2008/09 at The Gnoll

I realise that for some players – and dare I say supporters – they wouldn't care if they never set foot in The Gnoll again.

To outsiders, it could be a hostile, unforgiving little ground where a partisan crowd would always make life uncomfortable, in the sporting sense that is.

But for me, it will always be special as the ground where I took my first steps in top-flight rugby.

You simply don't get venues like The Gnoll in professional rugby these days, such is the necessity for corporate hospitality and all the trappings that go with the modern matchday experience.

That's a fact of life I suppose, but I for one miss the old grounds – and I miss The Gnoll.

When you ran out of the tunnel there was always a surge of raucous support from the main stand behind you.

The opposite side was fairly open, with the cricket pitch occupying a fairly vast piece of green space that rises gently up to Gnoll Country Park.

There was temporary seating put across that side in later years but the set-up took none of the atmosphere away from the place in my eyes.

Another source of tremendous noise was the Town Terrace behind the posts at the south side of the ground who at times would break into their famous 'Neath, Neath, Neath' chant.

And of course, what made The Gnoll great for me wasn't the fixtures and fittings of the place, it was the people who filled it.

In the days when I was just coming through I got such tremendous support from people who still to this day are backing me.

Back then, we'd often have a pint with the supporters in the clubhouse bar after games.

We'd always have a meal in the upstairs lounge and to get there you'd have to go through the bar downstairs and it was always brilliant to be able to mix with people and have a bit of banter about the game.

You don't get that sort of thing nowadays and I understand the reasons why the game has changed.

But those Gnoll days will always occupy a special place in my heart.

Loftus Versfled, Pretoria

I don't know, but there is something about this place that makes the hairs on the back of the neck stand on end.

I have never won there, but I did score a lovely try for Wales in a Test defeat to the Springboks in 2008.

It's just the atmosphere that it generates, and that at a venue with a capacity – 51,000 – that is far from enormous by the standards of today.

Welsh supporters are passionate, everyone knows that, but the South Africans run them close in my experience, especially when they congregate at Loftus.

The stadium is, of course, at altitude and so whenever we have played there we've spent some considerable time preparing for that.

It means that there's always a bit more trepidation when you run out at the place in anticipation of just how your body is going to cope with the thinner air that you know your opposition are far more used to.

Fortunately, I've never been too adversely affected by altitude, though it can cripple some players.

What I also love about this place is the dry deck that always awaits you there.

Like any winger, the firmer the ground, the more of a spring there is in my step.

James Hook takes in the scene at Loftus Versfeld

Suncorp Stadium, Brisbane

I've chosen this stadium primarily for the memory it holds of our 2003 World Cup quarter-final against England.

Sometimes you go to a ground and you just find that the place automatically agrees with you.

It's hard to expand more on that, but as a player you do sometimes get a liking for an arena that you can't put down to any logical reason.

The Suncorp is not dissimilar to the Millennium Stadium in the way its stands rise steeply from the bottom tier, giving that intimacy that players and spectators both appreciate.

I wouldn't mind someone lifting the Suncorp up and depositing it here in the UK!

Gareth Jenkins, then Wales coach, before a 2007 Test at the Suncorp

Ospreys host The Scarlets at the
Liberty Stadium in December 2010

Liberty Stadium, Swansea

When you're a rugby player, there's nothing like home –
which is why the Liberty Stadium will always be on my list
of favourite venues.

The Ospreys moved there for the start of the 2005/06
season having previously played at both The Gnoll and St
Helen's in Swansea, and it quickly began to feel like home.

My fondness for The Gnoll and grounds like it is one
thing, but the benefits you get as a player from being

able to play somewhere like the Liberty Stadium are too
numerous to mention. I love the pitch there, which we
obviously share with Swansea City Football Club and it is
one of the best surfaces to play on anywhere in the UK.

It gives me all the opportunity I could need to maximise
my speed and it seems to be in permanently good
condition, even at the height of winter when there are so
many games taking place on it.

SHANE'S TOP 10 TRIES

There were plenty to choose from but Shane managed to pick his 10 favourite tries. He describes how they came about and what they meant to him

Running clear to score one of his three tries against Cardiff

BIG BREAK

Neath v Cardiff (The Gnoll, September 1999)

This is one of my all-time favourite games as well, even though we lost, because I got what I consider to be one of the finest hat-tricks of my career.

One stood out. It came from a loose kick by Richard Wintle and I picked the ball up bobbling by our 22.

I just set off, beat about five or six men and went on my own to the line.

It was a huge boost to my confidence to do something like that against a team like Cardiff. I just thought to myself that from then on there was no reason why I couldn't keep doing that sort of thing.

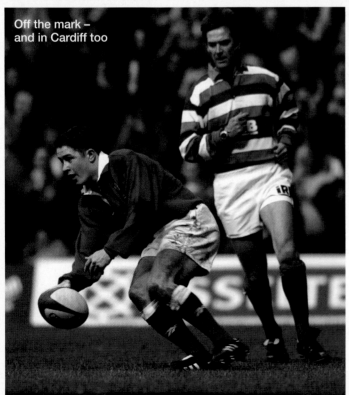

Off the mark – and in Cardiff too

FIRST OF MANY

Wales v Italy (Six Nations, Millennium Stadium, February 2000)

I have scored far better tries than this for my country but very few that have meant as much.

This was my very first score for my country and it came in a 47-16 win in front of our own fans in Cardiff.

A week earlier I had made my debut as a substitute against France and had a pass intercepted by Emile Ntamack that cost us a try.

So I was overjoyed to be selected to start against the Italians and the try was a sort of proof that the decision was correct.

We enjoyed a brilliant first half, at the end of which we were 30-9 ahead, and my try came after a steady build up of pressure and a beautifully weighted flat pass from centre Mark Taylor.

In the pictures of me scoring now I look like a little schoolboy. I felt like one at times in those early Wales years.

ARGENTINA BLITZ

Wales v Argentina
(Velez Sarsfield, June 2004)

It's not often you score three tries in the first half and your team are 25-0 up and seemingly out of sight at half-time.

But that is the situation we were in against Argentina on this particular occasion.

I went past their full-back to get it going, and then beat numerous men on the way to the line.

It was quite a feeling and it was as if I could have jinked through an entire army that day. I felt so light on my feet and so full of attacking intention.

I think it was the psychological effect it had on Argentina as well. They knew that no matter what they did in terms of a comeback, we had some real artillery in our side that day.

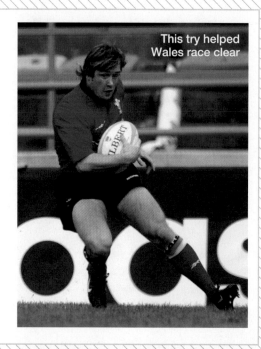

This try helped Wales race clear

A feeling of great satisfaction in the dressing room afterwards with Hal Luscombe and Sonny Parker

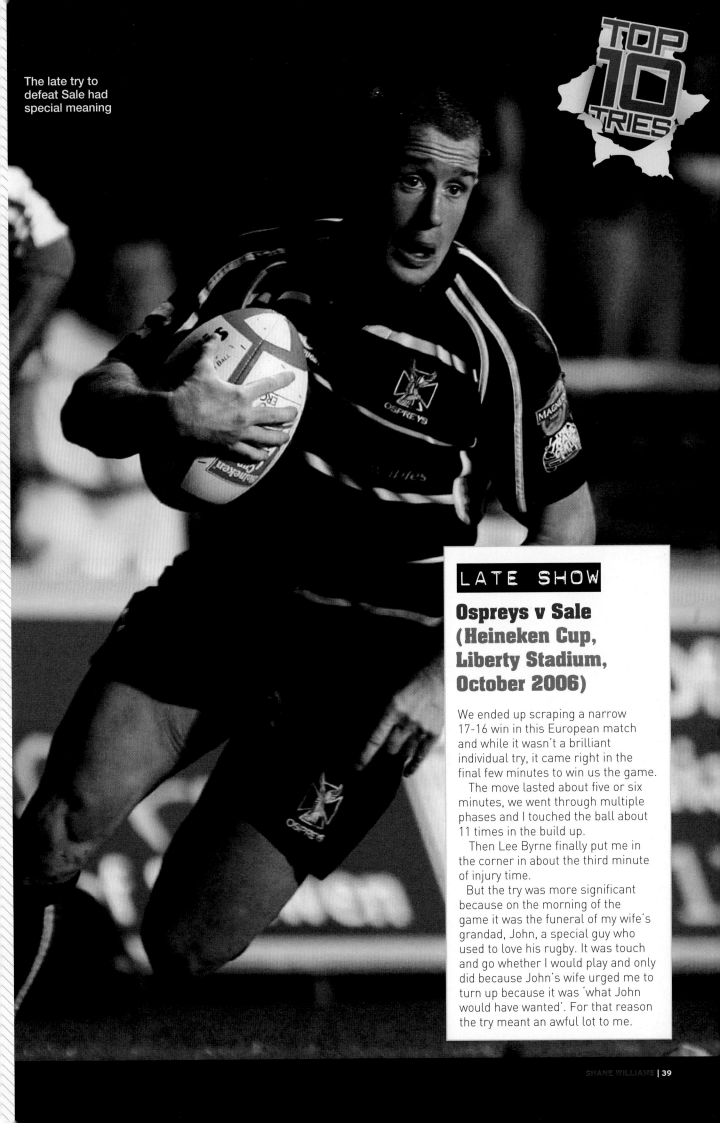

The late try to defeat Sale had special meaning

LATE SHOW

Ospreys v Sale (Heineken Cup, Liberty Stadium, October 2006)

We ended up scraping a narrow 17-16 win in this European match and while it wasn't a brilliant individual try, it came right in the final few minutes to win us the game.

The move lasted about five or six minutes, we went through multiple phases and I touched the ball about 11 times in the build up.

Then Lee Byrne finally put me in the corner in about the third minute of injury time.

But the try was more significant because on the morning of the game it was the funeral of my wife's grandad, John, a special guy who used to love his rugby. It was touch and go whether I would play and only did because John's wife urged me to turn up because it was 'what John would have wanted'. For that reason the try meant an awful lot to me.

SPRINT CLEAR

Wales v Fiji
(Rugby World Cup,
September 2007)

I just remember thinking as soon as I had the ball I
was going to score and I was proved right as barely a
defensive finger was laid on me.

It was quite a simple try as I took a pass from Tom
Shanklin and out-sprinted their cover defence wide out.

It was that sort of game, gaps and opportunities opening
up left, right and centre, although of course that ended up
not suiting us.

When I crossed the line I finished off with an
extravagant swallow dive a la Chris Ashton, which didn't
go down well with the critics afterwards who said the
occasion was inappropriate for such showboating.

With respect, I think they were taking it all a bit
seriously. I'm professional enough to know that there
is no risk of me dropping the ball in that situation.
Once I have the scent of a try in my nostrils that ball is
superglued to my hands.

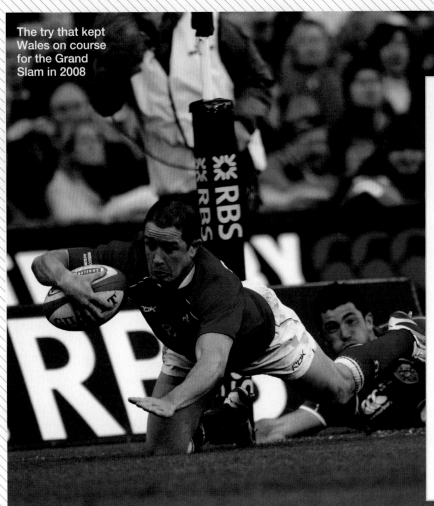

The try that kept Wales on course for the Grand Slam in 2008

HAND-OFF

Wales v Ireland (Croke Park, March 2008)

I haven't scored too many tries by handing someone off but that's what happened as I scooted through to claim the only try of the game in what was our fourth win out of five in the 2008 Grand Slam.

When I received the ball in the 50th minute, Ireland looked to have the situation covered, but I spotted the smallest of gaps and I think my acceleration caught one or two of their defenders off balance.

It was a score that ended up knocking the stuffing out of the home side even though it was tight all the way through.

After I touched the ball down I punched it into the first row of the stand in sheer delight.

GRAND SCORE

Wales v France (Millennium Stadium, March 2008)

This carried huge meaning because it was the one that saw me break Gareth Thomas's record of 40 tries for Wales.

That too came from a hack on and it was bouncing awkwardly as I went to ground it.

I felt like I had the whole of France chasing after me from behind as well, which didn't exactly make me feel settled.

But it was a day when everything went right and the bounce favoured me. On another day it might have been different.

It was a score that broke French resistance and we never looked back.

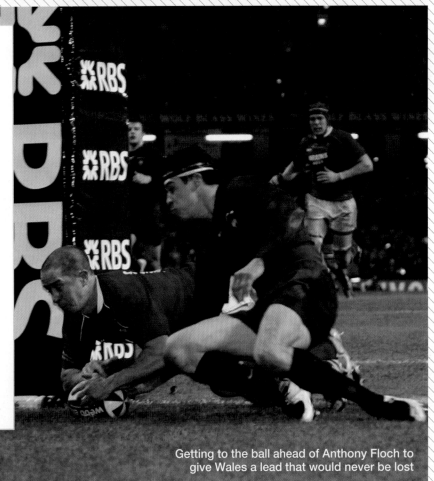

Getting to the ball ahead of Anthony Floch to give Wales a lead that would never be lost

HABANA & ME

Wales v South Africa first Test (Bloemfontein, June 2008)

By the time I went over for my first try of our 2008 tour to South Africa we were well beaten in the first Test and so the overall situation took some of the gloss off the score.

A long pass from James Hook found Mark Jones who in turn released to Morgan Stoddart who had come on as substitute at full-back. Morgan sucked in the last man and somehow freed me on the left.

It was the moment most of their media had been waiting for, me against the cross-field covering Bryan Habana. But I just stepped inside him and raced to the posts.

If that was at least something for Welsh fans to savour, the truth was it was much too little, too late.

Adrian Jacobs can't stop a fantastic score

Joy unconfined after a dizzying run produced a memorable try

TWIST & TURN

Wales v South Africa second Test (Loftus Versfeld, June 2008)

This is one of my very favourite scores, better easily than the one I scored in the first Test.

I pounced on a loose ball and got past their hooker John Smit first of all. I pinned my ears back and headed for the corner. I didn't think I could beat the cover defence by running in a straight line, but there was nobody to offload the ball to.

As I went to step inside, I realised the defender nearest to me had turned his head slightly and that if I changed my angle a bit I might just get there.

My instinct was correct, as soon as I stepped off my right foot and headed back towards the outside, I knew I was in.

And at least that try meant more in the context of the game, even if we did end up losing again.

Ospreys v London Irish (Heineken Cup, Liberty Stadium, October 2010)

This was a tight affair but a must-win match for us. It had been an attritional game up to the 52nd minute and our attempts to break out of defence were being thwarted by some well organised and belligerent Irish tackling.

But when we embarked on a breakout and I received the ball in midfield, I thought I'd try something different.

I chipped the ball over the advancing Irish back-line with the outside of my left foot and gave chase.

You make your own luck in these situations, but the ball bounced perfectly for me to scoop it up and the speed I had generated in the chase took me around a couple of players, allowing me to sprint all the way to the corner.

Saluting a try in the EDF Energy Cup semi-final win over Saracens at the Millennium Stadium

THE BEST OF TIMES

In 2008, Shane Williams was named IRB World Player of the Year and BBC Wales Sports Presonality of the Year as he inspired success for his country and the Ospreys. Tries and trophies flowed during a dazzling 12 months

Offloading under pressure from Australia's Phil Waugh

I suppose every player dreams about the sort of year I had in 2008.

I know I certainly did as a kid.

It's like when you're young and you play football in the park and imagine you're scoring the winner in the last minute of the FA Cup final.

You simply don't imagine any of the things that happened in that year actually happening to you, ever.

Not even after I had broken through into professional rugby did I see it coming, because for years when I was in the Neath team I doubted whether I'd end up staying the course.

Even when I was first picked for Wales I was too shy to mix with the established senior players like Scott Quinnell, Rob Howley and Scott Gibbs and used to hide away in my room when we got together as a squad.

I even thought about quitting back in 2001-2002 when a succession of injuries was dragging me down to the point when I thought it wasn't worth it.

I'm not the type to brag and will always acknowledge that I was only able to achieve what I did in 2008 because of my team-mates, but I did feel on top of the world.

In a way, I wasn't surprised that I at least was in good form as the year began because even though we had bombed out of the World Cup at the tail end of 2007,

Holding the Triple Crown plate after Ireland had been defeated at Croke Park

'The 2005 Grand Slam shocked us as a team, but in 2008 my own expectations were much higher'

Diving over the line to score in a 21-18 win over Australia in November

personally I had felt fitter and stronger than for some time.

Gareth Jenkins' departure meant Warren Gatland, Shaun Edwards and Rob Howley came in with a completely new broom for the start of 2008 – and the effect was immediate.

The boys responded at once to their brand of short, sharp training sessions, to Shaun's demand for perfection and training ground bark, and to Warren's steely organisational skills.

I remember Shaun shouting at me one time: "Get up on the front line!" as we did a defensive drill.

You know what, next time I made damn sure I got up on the front line.

If the 2005 Grand Slam had shocked even us as a team, in 2008 my own expectations were much higher.

I clearly remember leaving the field at half-time of the first Six Nations match against England at Twickenham when we were 16-6 down thinking to myself: "Why are we losing to this lot? We're better than them."

The rest, as they say, is history. We came out like men possessed in that second half and won for the first time in 20 years at Headquarters. We never looked back.

I felt I had a relatively quiet game against the old enemy, but thereafter I just came to life.

I got in on the try-scoring act in a 47-8 win against Italy the following game, claimed two more against the Scots in a 30-15 success and then the fourth, pivotal, encounter was upon us away to Ireland.

That was a huge test because they had proved our nemesis in Dublin too often, but I squeezed through for the

Celebrating victory over Australia with Lee Byrne, who also scored a try that afternoon

'What a year. The greatest of my life. I felt like I was on an unstoppable roll'

match-winning score early in the second half and we took the honours 16-12.

The final outing, on a damp day in Cardiff at home to the French, was a special game in so many ways.

We won, I scored – and it was a try that took me past Gareth Thomas's all-time Welsh record of 40.

A summer tour to South Africa followed, and although we lost both Tests, which was a source of huge frustration, there were some personal highlights yet again.

All tour their media were asking me about my duel with former world player of the year Bryan Habana; to be honest I got fed up with it in the end.

But while we lost both games against the Boks 43-17 and 37-21, I did score twice against the great man; the try in the second match, which put us 15-14 ahead after half an hour, being a real peach.

I picked the ball up off a scrum near the halfway line and jinked my way home to grab one of the most satisfying scores ever.

The year continued with a fine home win against

Australia that November, when I claimed another try, but there were some very special individual accolades to take stock of too.

For a start, to be given the man of the tournament award for the Six Nations was a real honour.

Martyn Williams had won it in 2005 and he must have been close in 2008 as well, such was his contribution.

But I was called up to the committee room one morning after Ospreys training to be told I'd won it, and it was another box I could tick in what was turning out to be an incredible year.

But the biggest endorsement of what we'd done, and I say 'we' because it felt very much to me like an award for the whole team, was winning the IRB World Player of the Year award in November.

No Welshman had ever received it and you only had to look at the past winners – Habana, Richie McCaw, Jonny Wilkinson, Schalk Burger etc – to realise the prestige of it.

I went with Ryan Jones, who was also shortlisted, to the ceremony in London and when they read out my name my heart was pounding.

It's something that can't ever be taken away from me.

Finally, at the BBC Wales Sports Personality of the Year do, I was crowned again, going next to names like Joe Calzaghe, Ryan Giggs and Colin Jackson on the trophy.

What a year. The greatest of my life.

I felt like I was on an unstoppable roll, that no opponent could get the better of me and that if I tried something it was always going to come off.

Nine times out of 10 in 2008, it did.

PRIDE OF THE LIONS

Shane's tours with the British and Irish Lions have brought highs and frustrations, although the 2009 trip to South Africa was the best of his life

2005 (New Zealand)

It might not have been a successful tour, but I did take a lot from our 2005 trip to New Zealand under the command of Clive Woodward. It was the hardest rugby I have ever played in my life.

We were taught a humiliating lesson in the Test series by Graham Henry's All Blacks, losing 3-0 and never remotely looking like winning any of them.

And the personal disappointment for me was that I only figured in the second Test – a 48-18 hammering at the Westpac Stadium in Wellington. I wasn't chosen for the first Test and I missed the last one because of a minor back injury.

The Welsh boys benefited that year because of course we had won the Grand Slam, so we were bang in form with many of us having impressed Woodward.

I was reasonably confident of getting the nod for the squad but I never count my chickens. The day we were due to hear was a nervous one.

I found out while we were travelling home from an Ospreys match against Connacht in Galway.

We were expecting to be told via text message but we were sitting in the departure lounge of Shannon Airport watching Sky Sports News and the infobar was saying 'Lions squad to be announced shortly'. I thought we'd missed out.

Then sure enough, the bleep-bleep was heard and a message read on my phone: 'Congratulations, you have been selected for the British and Irish Lions in New Zealand. Clive'.

It was a great moment, but the feeling of elation didn't compare to when I was first selected for Wales by Graham Henry.

When we met up, I had similar feelings to the ones I had experienced when I first became a Wales player, though not as bad. What I mean is that the presence of World Cup-winning players like Lawrence Dallaglio, Richard Hill, Jason Robinson and the Irish captain Brian O'Driscoll was slightly intimidating.

Despite the size of the squad, which was the biggest ever, there were very few egos and we got on really well.

One night, as part of team bonding we had to split up into groups and perform sketches. Some of the guys

Gareth Thomas scores a try in the second Test against New Zealand in 2005

Offloading during the second Test at Wellington, his only appearance in the 2005 series

revelled in it, others were deeply embarrassed, me included!

We were very scratchy in a warm-up game against Argentina in Cardiff before we left with Jonny Wilkinson rescuing a draw for us with a late penalty.

One of the first things I noticed when we met up were the sheer number of coaches that were big names in themselves even though they were not the head coach. There was Andy Robinson, Gareth Jenkins, Eddie O'Sullivan, and the whole management group added up to a staggering 26 people.

It was quite hard at times to get used to the number of different messages that were being conveyed.

The first Test will always be remembered for the spear tackle that ended O'Driscoll's tour cruelly, Tana Umaga and Kevan Mealamu the perpetrators. My view is that it was dangerous play, no question and the camera doesn't really lie on that score. But I do not believe Brian was consciously targeted beforehand.

I was disappointed not to figure in that game but I wasn't going to sulk and after we lost 21-3 there was a clamour for change that worked in my favour.

I was chosen to play left wing in the second Test, by which time Gareth Thomas had taken over as captain from the stricken O'Driscoll.

Alfie brought a humour and a vibrancy to the squad through his unique personality, but he couldn't turn the tide on his own. After he went over for an early try in Wellington, the All Blacks hit back to thrash us.

We had the best players Britain and Ireland could muster, but we were no match for the skill, organisation and power that they threw at us. As far as I am concerned that All Black side was the best there has ever been, even if they didn't win the World Cup.

What took my breath away was their winning attitude, there was just no way they were ever going to lose those games and they played harder than they had probably ever played to make sure of it.

Physically, I was battered in that game. I was hit hard when I had the ball and I took a fair few digs when I didn't have it.

I've played in South Africa, Argentina, Italy, places where you know you are going to take some punishment, but I had never encountered such a devastating mix of physicality, high standard of play and will to win.

When I knew I was going to miss the last Test I went with Gordon D'Arcy, Chris Cusiter, Gavin Henson and Gareth Cooper to Queenstown to let off some steam.

We drank a lot, had next to no sleep and ended up doing a bungee jump that scared the living daylights out of me.

All in all, I don't think that tour worked. The party was too big, we never developed a Test team capable of holding its own and the whole trip ended up being a mixed experience for me.

I went home thinking I had unfinished business with the Lions, there were so many things unfulfilled.

Fortunately I had the chance to take care of that in 2009 – though again disappointment reigned.

Gareth Thomas runs at the All Black defence during the first Test in Christchurch in 2005

2009 (South Africa)

It might have been a tour that ended in a gutting 2-1 series defeat, but it will go down as the best trip of my life.

I shall always look back on it with brilliant memories, though I never went into it on the high that I had gone into New Zealand in 2005.

In 2008 my stock as a player had never been so high, it was almost as if everything I touched turned to gold.

But by the time the summer of 2009 arrived I had just finished a season where I had struggled for consistency with the Ospreys and Wales.

I didn't feel I was playing badly, and so to get the call for the Lions for the second time was a huge fillip, especially as some were questioning my worth.

I try not to pay attention to negative press because I am my own harshest critic anyway. But I would be lying if I said it doesn't get to you and niggle at the back of your mind.

There were question marks against me because I hadn't lit up the

Six Nations like I had done the year before, but the truth was I had not been 100 per cent since picking up an ankle injury in our first match against Scotland at Murrayfield.

After that, everything became a struggle, though by the time the Lions squad was due to be announced I felt I was getting back to better form.

This time, we heard at the same time as the general public, via Sky Sports News rather than a personal text message, which was a method I felt was far more uncomplicated and sensible.

I honestly always believed I would be picked despite the doom-mongers saying otherwise and so it was on to Pennyhill Park in Surrey to meet up with the squad at the hotel where England always base themselves.

There was no formal meet up, more a case of gradually seeing the guys around the place as you settled in and introducing yourself.

Whether Ian McGeechan paid attention to players' personalities in his selection I don't know, but the chemistry of the group was brilliant from the world go. Everyone got on so well, even guys who were vying for the same position.

For example, I got on great with Ugo Monye, who was a rival for the wing's position, but everyone was so down to earth.

Shaun Edwards, the Wales defence coach who was on the trip, told me not pay any attention to the critics as we left for South Africa, but to just trust in my ability and he was a great source of reassurance. But I was worried about my form and my confidence was low.

In the first match against a Royal XV I was desperate to make an impression and run in a few tries, but it just wouldn't happen for me. To make things worse I dropped the ball over the line as I went to score which is something I can't ever remember doing elsewhere.

On top of that I passed the ball into touch at one stage and every time we got ourselves into a promising position we either bombed possession or the ball didn't come my way.

Afterwards I was very frustrated, beating myself up about the way things had gone.

I had a few other run outs but it was the same old story and once, after a clash against the Sharks, I can recall going back to my room, looking in the mirror and physically slapping myself in the face to try and snap myself out of it.

I'm not saying that it worked but something seemed to click after that.

I didn't get selected for the first Test, Ugo got the nod, but in a way I wasn't too devastated because I was expecting it.

I was more focused on trying to think positively and regain some form which I felt was happening.

Losing the first Test was a blow, but the way we came back later in the game was a boost to everybody, the 26-21 final scoreline far more respectable than had once looked the case.

The second Test in Durban will go down as one of the most memorable and brutal contests in the history of the Lions.

'I can recall looking in the mirror and physically slapping myself in the face to try and snap myself out of it'

Both Adam Jones and Gethin Jenkins went off early in the second half because of injury and they ended up winning it with a last-minute Morne Steyn penalty.

The controversial factor was the referee's failure to send off Schalk Burger for what appeared to be a blatant act of eye gouging on Luke Fitzgerald in the opening stages.

I like Schalk as a player and a person and anything like that would have been very out of character, but perhaps we should have gone on to win that game without needing them to be down to 14 men.

The tour finished on a high for me as I ran in two tries in the third Test, albeit a dead rubber.

South Africa 2009 had failed to yield the glory that it could, and perhaps should have done.

But the experience, the friendships I made with players from other countries and the opportunity to work with a great coach like Ian McGeechan is something I will always be grateful for.

Ian McGeechan, who Shane describes as a "great coach", led the 2009 Lions in South Africa

MY TOUGHEST OPPONENTS

During over a decade at the top of his sport, these are the men he has competed against who have made the biggest impression on Shane

Jason Robinson

I was lucky enough to play alongside Jason on the 2005 Lions tour and I can assure you I would rather play with him than against him.

He was one of those players who seemed to get better with age and when he decided to retire after the 2007 World Cup, England were the weaker for his absence.

Great players for me are one-offs, guys who can almost offer things that no-one else can.

Jason fell into that category.

He was one of the most devastating counter-attackers the game has ever seen. His ability to step off either foot at blistering pace just took your breath away at times.

All this from a player who came from rugby league. You'd never have known that because he made the switch with consummate ease, making it look as if he was born to play union.

All this and Jason was one hell of a nice guy too. I found that out on the Lions tour.

Tana Umaga

I was never in direct opposition to him because he was a centre, but what a player.

My admiration for him was bolstered by the way he performed for the All Blacks when we were there with the Lions in 2005.

Don't get me wrong, Tana has caused Wales plenty of damage down the years, but on that tour his work-rate, class and dynamism were amazing. He simply never stopped running during games.

Umaga would be the first to put his body on the line in any given situation but he was also a master at exploiting opportunities in attack.

Paul O'Connell

Now I'm not going to claim to be an expert on second row play, but I've seen enough of this guy in my time

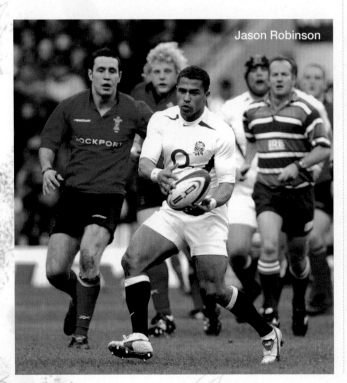

Jason Robinson

Tana Umaga

Paul O'Connell

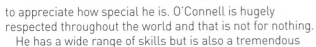
Doug Howlett

Richard Hill tackling Gavin Henson

to appreciate how special he is. O'Connell is hugely respected throughout the world and that is not for nothing.

He has a wide range of skills but is also a tremendous ball-carrier and very aggressive to go with it.

Aside from that though, he is just a huge man, the kind you never want to have running at you at pace on a rugby field.

His will to win seeps through his every pore as well. Look how many times he has got Ireland or Munster out of tight corners.

Richard Hill

Retired now, but one of the best back row forwards I have ever had the misfortune to play against.

When I saw him at close quarters on the Lions tour of 2005 he was probably past his best.

However his dedication, professionalism and will to win still came roaring through in everything he did.

Sir Clive Woodward once singled him out as the best player he had ever worked with and that doesn't surprise me at all.

Hill was one of the pivotal reasons why Saracens turned over the Ospreys against the odds in the Heineken Cup quarter-final of 2008, a defeat that still rankles.

Doug Howlett

I've faced him a number of times and he's always been someone I have admired.

He had blistering pace and a high skill level that you would expect of a test calibre wing, but I always thought he read the game brilliantly and it is no surprise that he has doubled up as a full-back in his time.

Howlett was a master at knowing how to finish off moves, he had an antennae that always seemed to lead him into the right gaps.

And he was also a guy who never seemed not to be involved even though he was on the wing. Just a great player.

Martyn Williams

While Martyn has more often been a team-mate of mine with Wales and the Lions (thank goodness), I've included him here because I know too what a menace he is to play against.

I've faced him numerous times for the Ospreys against the Blues and on his day, he just seems to be everywhere, his work-rate is phenomenal.

Martyn's strength is also game-awareness and being able to read situations in attack and defence.

So often he'll pop in just the right place at the right time to hurt the opposition.

And he has a fierce will to win as well.

THE GRAND SLAMS

The glorious era of Gerald Davies, Phil Bennett and Gareth Edwards came to a triumphant end with the 1978 Grand Slam. It would be another 27 years before the nation could rejoice again as the class of 2005 swept all before them, while the feat was repeated in 2008. Shane talks us through each game

2005

Gavin Henson's winning penalty with five minutes left. The inset photo shows Shane outpacing Mark Cueto to score one of his most important tries

CARDIFF BOUNCES

Wales 11 England 9

We'd been building towards this since returning from the 2003 World Cup with a spring in our step having put in great displays against New Zealand and England.

The Six Nations of 2004 was so-so, but in the autumn of that year we ran New Zealand close, eventually losing by a point in a nip-and-tuck 26-25 defeat.

By the time England rolled into town we felt we were ready to claim the scalp of the then world champions.

It was a nervy affair. I went over in the left corner for the only try of the game in the first half, but Charlie Hodgson's penalties kept them in touch to the point that with less then 10 minutes left they were edging it 9-8.

Enter Gavin Henson to take a kick that would shape the next five years or so of his career. His long-range penalty took real guts under pressure, and as soon as he hit it I felt it was going over.

We tried to keep a lid on the celebrations afterwards because we had a week's turnaround before facing Italy in Rome. But I don't mind admitting that it was difficult. Cardiff was bouncing that night.

Dodging the Italian defence for a superb team try

TOTAL RUGBY

Italy 8 Wales 38

Whenever you go to Italy you are confronted with talk about banana skins and how Stadio Flaminio is no longer an easy place to go.

It's all true, the Azzurri are not the pushovers they once were, but going into this one we were on fire.

I remember making an early break up the middle of the field and thinking to myself that this was going to be a game of chances. It was.

After some cagey stuff in the first half we really cut loose to run in six tries, one by yours truly after some brilliant link up play.

We showed that day that we had cast off the shackles of self-doubt.

They called our brand of play 'Total Rugby' in some quarters, in homage to the Dutch football team of the Seventies. A style like that was always going to suit me.

An outburst of emotion as referee Paul Honiss blows the final whistle. A superb defensive effort kept France at bay in the closing minutes

PARIS COMEBACK

France 18 Wales 24

We were so badly pummelled in the first-half that by the time we trooped off at the interval I could scarcely believe we were only trailing 15-6.

I'd been steamrollered by their big winger Aurelien Rougerie, but the dressing room was where our coach Mike Ruddock came into his own.

He rallied us, saying that we had so much more to give and this game was there for the taking. Seeing my confidence had taken a knock he told me to go out and show what I was made of. His speech worked. Martyn Williams got two quick tries to put us ahead and we dug deep to hold on.

In the final few minutes France needed a converted try and it felt like the entire nation was trying to get it. But our defending was sublime and we held out for what I class as one of the best victories I have ever had the pleasure to be involved in. It was the pivotal win of the campaign.

HYMNS & ARIAS IN EDINBURGH

Scotland 22 Wales 46

Murrayfield traditionally presents problems for Wales. Not this time.

Come half-time we were an extraordinary 38-3 ahead with the home side in complete disarray.

We hit them hard early on by continuing with our pass and move, high tempo style.

Ryan Jones went over in the first few minutes after a flowing move; me, Kevin Morgan – who was in for broken thumb victim Gareth Thomas – and Rhys Williams followed him.

It was a rout that had the Welsh hordes singing hymns and arias long before the final whistle.

We stepped off the gas as the game wore on, and Scottish pride made the score more respectable.

But it was job done. Now only Ireland stood in our way.

Running in to score one of five first-half tries for Wales

Rhys Williams strolls in for another five points

Above: Kevin Morgan shows his joy after scoring, while, below, the whole squad get the bubbly out in the dressing room afterwards

HANGOVER FROM HELL

Wales 32 Ireland 20

We were back home for the final fling, and when I drew the curtains of my hotel room on the morning of the game a bright blue sky and glorious spring sunshine greeted me.

I somehow knew there and then that this was going to be our day.

By this time, given the rugby we had produced beforehand, it seemed the whole of Wales thought the same way. It was one of those days when defeat is unimaginable.

Don't forget, we were up against a superb Irish side that day, but we had the momentum of a runaway train.

Gethin Jenkins got us off to a great start with a charge-down try and by the time a lovely flat pass from Tom Shanklin put Kevin Morgan over midway through the second half, our first Grand Slam in 27 years was in the bag.

That night WAS the time to celebrate.

We went to a pub in the grounds of the Brains Brewery in the centre of Cardiff and toasted what had been an incredible campaign.

The next morning I was due to speak to the press but I woke up with the hangover from hell and didn't make it!

But it was one hangover worth having.

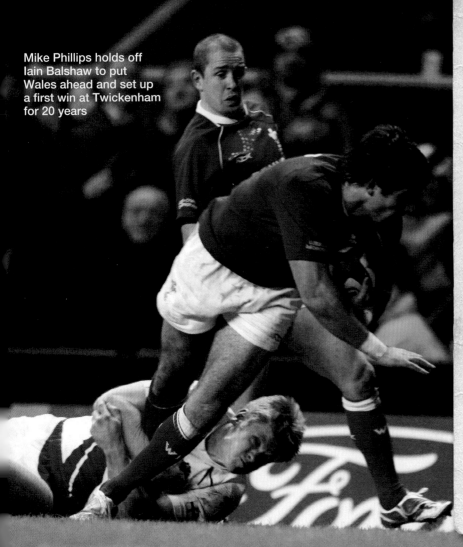

Mike Phillips holds off Iain Balshaw to put Wales ahead and set up a first win at Twickenham for 20 years

2008

ARMS ALOFT

England 19 Wales 26

I always think of Huw Bennett, our hooker, when I recall this game. Were it not for his try-saving tackle on Paul Sackey just before half-time, I'm not sure we'd have ended a 20-year hoodoo at Twickenham.

Huw's tackle ensured the half-time deficit was only 16-6. Had another converted try gone on top of that, the mountain would have been too high.

As it was, we knew we were as good as England. A blistering second half proved it. Lee Byrne and Mike Phillips went over for the key scores and the good thing was that we didn't finish the game hanging on. Instead we were camped on their line.

When the whistle blew there were more than a few arms in red jerseys held aloft. It was an incredible first match for our new coaching duo of Warren Gatland and Shaun Edwards.

Talk about a new broom!

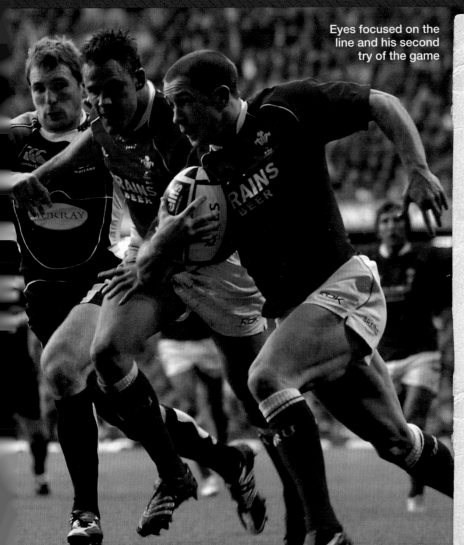

Eyes focused on the line and his second try of the game

TOUCH AND GO

Wales 30 Scotland 15

While the final scoreline looks emphatic, the match was anything but for long periods.

We were only 10-6 in front at half-time but gradually we began to make our class tell.

The match will always be remembered for a rather controversial decision that went in my favour in the second half. When I received the ball in a good midfield position I sniffed a gap out wide on the left and decided to pin my ears back.

My Ospreys colleague Nikki Walker ended up as the last defender as I lunged for the corner.

There was an anxious wait before the television official ruled that I had neither put my foot in touch or touched the corner flag in the process of scoring.

And by this time that precious commodity of momentum was building once again. We couldn't do the Slam again...could we?

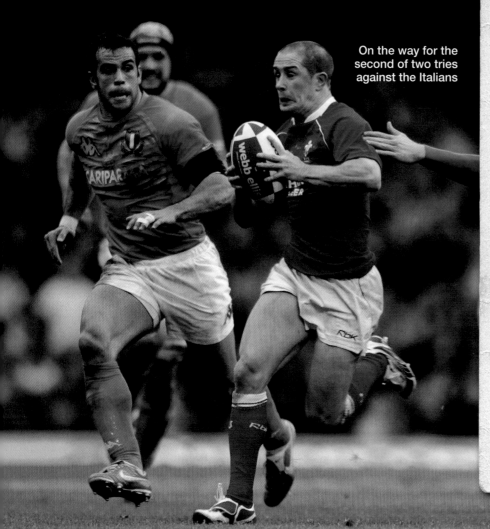

On the way for the second of two tries against the Italians

AT THE DOUBLE

Wales 47 Italy 8

Again, this was not as straightforward as the final score may suggest, but in the end once we cut loose we just had too much attacking threat for our visitors to cope.

Me and Lee Byrne helped ourselves to two tries each, Tom Shanklin got the other and Stephen Jones sent over 18 points via the boot.

I don't say this lightly but all the players felt we could lose this game going into it. In the times we have struggled against Italy in the past we have been dragged down to their level.

In this one we dictated the pattern and earned the right to play.

We knew if we did that and stayed patient the gaps would appear. And when they did, we took full advantage.

DUBLIN DELIGHT

Ireland 12 Wales 16

The fourth match of the campaign but arguably the pivotal one.

We went to Dublin amid the background of the press trying to whip up bad-feeling between the two coaches, Warren and Eddie O'Sullivan, who apparently had history from their time working in the Irish set-up.

But none of that really registered with us.

When you consider that we had two players – Mike Phillips and Martyn Williams – sin-binned at critical stages of this game, it's all the more remarkable that we came through to win it.

If we had played champagne stuff in the previous two fixtures, this was one where he had to be pragmatic and grind the victory out.

With the forwards to the fore, particularly our captain Ryan Jones who was quite magnificent, we pulled through for a hugely significant win that was sealed with a long-range James Hook penalty.

My try in the early stages of the second half was key as well, as I scooted through a small gap for a touchdown that gave me real pleasure.

Only France now stood in our way.

A clenched fist demonstrates what this try meant

James Hook lands a match-sealing penalty

The try-scorers in an embrace with Gavin Henson

Stephen Jones kicked 10 points against France

RECORD BREAKERS

Wales 29 France 12

If the morning of the 2005 Grand Slam game had been one of glorious sunshine, this time it was cloudy and drizzly and I did wonder if it was some sort of omen.

But I am not really that superstitious.

All the preparation work had been done, confidence was high, and I knew there was no reason for us not to come through.

The journey to the ground was nerve-wracking, once again I sensed the people in Cardiff's streets weren't contemplating defeat.

That was worrying because you never know what you're going to get with France.

But second half tries from me – the one that saw me break Gareth Thomas's 40-try Wales record – and Martyn Williams got us over the line.

It was fitting that Martyn had the last word because yet again he'd had a brilliant campaign, just like 2005.

In lots of ways it was one of the most improbable Slams of modern times because after our flop at the World Cup the previous year, nobody really gave us a prayer.

But Warren and his team pressed all the right buttons and got us to believe.

And it's amazing what you can achieve when you have belief.

For the second time in three seasons, Wales have completed the Grand Slam. Time for another party

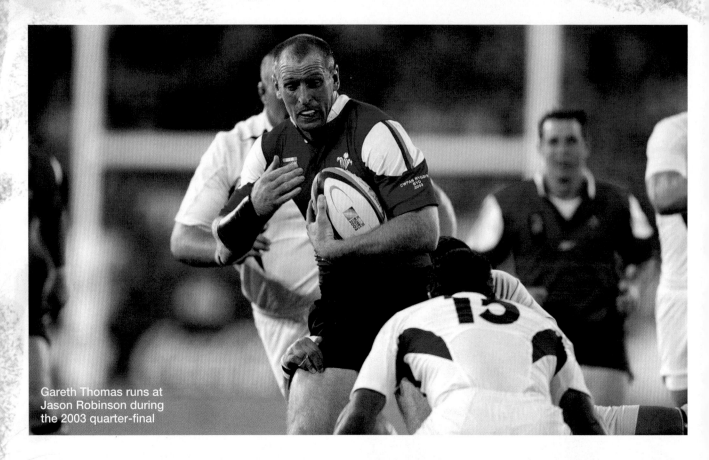

Gareth Thomas runs at Jason Robinson during the 2003 quarter-final

TAKING ON THE WORLD

Shane's two World Cups were contrasting experiences. In 2003 his dazzling performances invigorated Wales but four years later there was an early exit

2003

I went to Australia in 2003 having gotten into the squad by the skin of my teeth.

For a long time during his tenure between early 2002 and the summer of 2004, Steve Hansen just didn't seem to rate me.

At first, I was injured and out of form, and he had every reason not to select me. But when I came out of those doldrums and started to play like my true self, I just couldn't get myself on his radar. For a while I took the rejection personally and was a bit childish about it all.

I don't know whether he didn't trust my lack of size, but by the time the World Cup came around in 2003, I was sweating on making the travelling party.

Steve called me in one day shortly before he was due to make the announcement and I feared the worst, I thought he was about to try to let me down gently.

Instead, he wanted to know whether I'd be willing to go to the tournament as third choice scrum-half behind Dwayne Peel and Gareth Cooper.

Part of me thought 'you cheeky git!' but of course, I just wanted to be involved and so indicated that I'd be happy to fill the requirement.

I'd played number nine in the early days for Amman United and once or twice for Neath. Steve had it in mind

Fighting for the ball with Lawrence Dallagio

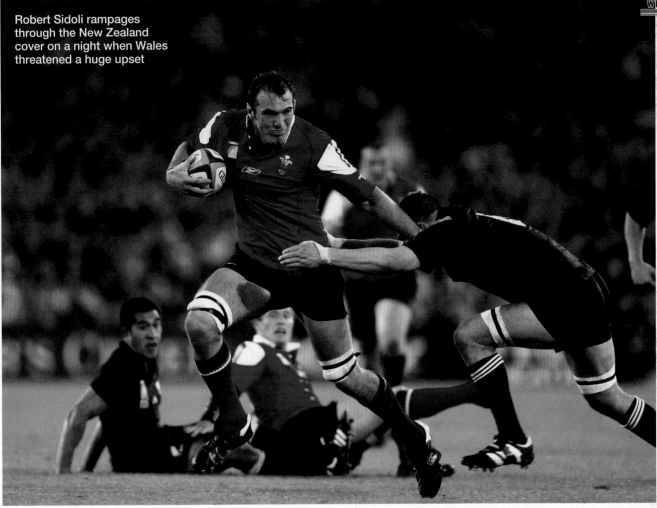

Robert Sidoli rampages through the New Zealand cover on a night when Wales threatened a huge upset

obviously that I could cover three positions, both wings and scrum-half, and that was probably what got me the nod.

But by the time we got on the plane, and in the first few weeks of the tour, I felt like little more than the baggage man.

In training it was clear that I didn't figure anywhere near the first team plans because I was always lined up in the opposition side that was meant to test those who were going to play in the pool matches against Canada, Tonga and Italy.

One day Steve gave me a rollicking when I ran the ball back instead of kicking it and I lost my head, telling him where to go in front of the other lads.

He took it, but then later warned me never to speak to him like that again.

I thought I'd burned my bridges, but then in the final pool match, once we were already guaranteed to reach the quarter-finals, I got my chance on the wing against New Zealand.

People were predicting the All Blacks might achieve three figures on the scoreboard, but it turned out to be

one of the most inspiring nights in the history of the Welsh team.

Sure, we didn't win – we lost 53-37 – but we shook them to the core and played our part in a wonderful game at the Telstra Stadium in Sydney.

I'd been in bed with the 'flu in the days leading up to the game and feared the worst, but when I got out there I just decided to bury the frustration of the last few weeks and go out and give it a whirl.

The rest is history. I popped up everywhere in the game, the ball seemed to find me all the time and the pitch seemed 15 yards wider than usual on both flanks.

Afterwards we drew some glowing plaudits and I made a point of telling the press that I hoped I'd proved a few doubters wrong.

I certainly seemed to make an impression on Steve because I never looked back after that under his command.

I played in the quarter-final against England the following week at the Suncorp Stadium in Brisbane, and although we lost to a team that were very much on their way to the top of the world, we once again did ourselves proud by giving Clive Woodward's team a real scare. Had we converted the two tries we scored in the first half that night it may even have turned into a fairytale for us.

But they gradually got themselves back into it in the second half, mainly through Jonny Wilkinson's penalties and that was that.

We were flying home, but very much with the feeling that a new dawn was about to break for the Wales team. It did in a way because from then until we won the Grand Slam in 2005, we stayed very much on the upward curve.

'Afterwards I made a point of telling the press that I hoped I'd proved a few doubters wrong'

RUGBY
WORLD CUP
2007

NANTES

Matthew Rees reaches
for the try-line against Fiji

2007

Going into the 2007 World Cup, we were struggling results-wise but I felt as fit and as strong as I had ever done.

I had clocked 4.66 seconds over 40 metres and was lifting heavier weights than usual. I was convinced I was in for a great World Cup personally.

But the indications for the team weren't good at all.

We were trounced by 60 points in a humiliating encounter against England at Twickenham and France beat us 34-7 at the Millennium Stadium.

It meant we were being all but written off as contenders in France and I suppose you couldn't blame the press or the punters for that.

It was a tough time for the coaching team of Gareth Jenkins and Nigel Davies. We were poor in the Six Nations that year, only salvaging some pride with a 28-17 win against England in the final game.

And that meant Gareth and Nigel were always under pressure. A lot of people held them personally responsible for what happened to us at the World Cup, but we players were the ones to blame.

I enjoyed working with Gareth and Nigel, I thought their methods were good and I didn't sense any disharmony among the squad. What I appreciated was that they gave me a free role, licence to roam and to get the ball in my hands as often as possible without having to worry too much about sticking to a rigid structure.

The trouble was more down to a lack of confidence because of our results. And if anything, perhaps the players were given too much opportunity to have input into what we were doing. I sometimes felt there were too many ideas being thrown into the pot from players and management and that led to a bit of confusion.

We got wins against Canada and Japan and lost the big one to Australia at the Millennium Stadium, 32-20, which was an afternoon when we were really disappointing.

It meant we needed to beat Fiji in Nantes to qualify and what unfolded was farcical at times. We lost 38-34 because we got sucked into an open, free-running basketball style of game, right up the Fijians' street.

In the dressing room afterwards we kind of knew that Gareth's days were numbered as coach and he was sacked the following morning before we had even left our base in La Baule, which disappointed me.

The mood was horrendous on the trip home, some of the lads just wanted to drown their sorrows.

When we reached the Vale Resort, our headquarters on the outside of Cardiff, Gareth got off the bus on his own a couple of hundred yards away from the hotel and it was a really sad way for him to depart.

Gareth had addressed us as a squad before we left La Baule and for such a proud man to leave us in the way he did was demoralising for me. My heart went out to him.

When he took the national job he was the logical choice, the man everyone believed had earned the chance after he had been passed over when Mike Ruddock was appointed.

But it was one of life's cruel twists that the job he had waited all his life to do never worked out. What happened would, I am sure, have been very difficult for him to deal with. The players found it difficult enough.

It was a dismal World Cup, the sort I hope I never have to experience again.

Above: Colin Charvis attempts to break free of Fiji's Sisa Koyamaibole, while, below, despair sets in as defeat means Wales are heading home after the group stage

Phil Waugh can't stop him but Wales lost to Australia

A spectacular dive for the line in a 42-17 win over Canada

WING WIZARDS

They are the entertainers and Shane is among the best of the breed. He tells us about other great wingers and what is required to succeed in the position

When it comes to what makes a great winger, there will be all sorts of different opinions from the great and the good in the game.

But there are also certain things that you can't really do without.

For a start, and this is probably the most obvious to everyone, you do need a bit of pace, the more the better in all honesty.

In football terms you are the striker in the team and you need speed to get you into the right positions and to enable you to take chances when they come your way.

Pace unsettles defenders, they fear it, it forces them to make mistakes and lose balance. It is a deadly weapon for any player to have.

But wing play is not all about running into space and feeling the breeze in your ears.

All the best wingers look for work, they look to stay as involved as they can even though that often demands that they pop up in all sorts of places around the field, at first receiver, in midfield, and on the opposite wing if needs be.

The trick is to be in receipt of the final pass and that requires an ability to read the game.

It is about having an instinct that enables you to anticipate what it going to happen before it actually does.

For example, James Hook is a player I find I have an almost telepathic understanding with at times.

In our win against Scotland at Murrayfield in this year's RBS Six Nations, Hooky made a break in the opening minutes and I was on his left shoulder to take a pass that gave me a simple run-in try.

But the key was that I knew he was going to make that break a split second before he did so.

I saw the situation unfold and we were clearly thinking the same thing.

From an opposition point of view, Doug Howlett is a player I admire hugely. He used to work off players in the New Zealand team to devastating effect.

It wasn't about Howlett being on a field and running rings around opposing defenders, much more about his game intelligence, his knowledge of when to hit a gap and when not to and his appreciation of everything that was around him. Howlett is always hungry for tries, like a predator. I too always found that the more tries I scored, the hungrier I played.

Doug Howlett had excellent "game intelligence" and was aware of everything that was going on around him

'James Hook is a player I find I have an almost telepathic understanding with at times'

Another player I admired was Christophe Dominici, the French international. He would work ever so hard off the centres and score a lot of tries because of that.

The worst wingers are the ones who glue themselves to the touchline and complain about poor service. If nothing is happening, then it is up to you to make it happen.

The best example I can give you is that if you were to look closely at all the tries scored by wingers in a given season, I bet you would be staggered by how many are not scored in the corners.

The classic image of a guy sliding in next to the corner flag is misleading in the modern game. Of course it still happens now and again, but much less so nowadays.

Dominici was so difficult to mark because he would appear in places you never expected and I always found Jason Robinson, the former England flier, to be equally as awkward to monitor.

Jason played in all kinds of positions; he had terrific feet, always got in the right place at the right time and made very few mistakes.

His game was founded on hard work; he made things look easy when they weren't.

I always found that players like the Tuilagi brothers, as good as they are at what they do, were easier to play against.

That's not to say that I enjoyed having them run at me

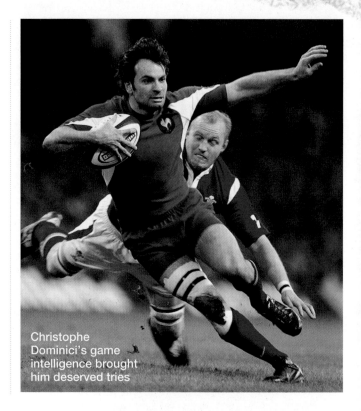

Christophe Dominici's game intelligence brought him deserved tries

'Dominici was so difficult to mark because he would appear in places you never expected and I always found Jason Robinson, the former England flier, to be equally as awkward to monitor'

Jason Robinson made the game look easy but only because of his hard work

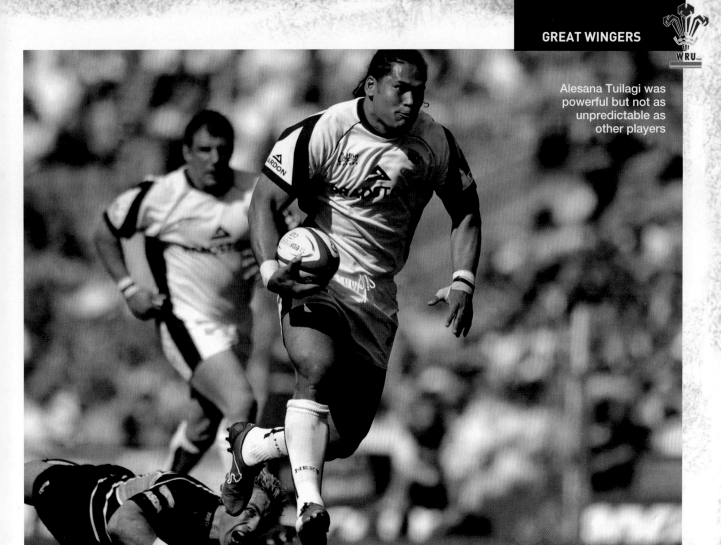

Alesana Tuilagi was powerful but not as unpredictable as other players

in space! But because of their power they looked to be put into places where they could make their size count in physical mis-matches.

The ones I hated playing against were the guys who when you looked up weren't where you expected them to be because they had gone off somewhere else looking to make nuisances of themselves.

There are two Welsh wingers in particular who I admire through my time playing – Gareth Thomas and Mark Jones. Gareth, or Alfie as everyone knows him, was not your classic winger and was versatile enough to be able to play at centre and full-back.

You just cannot argue with what he achieved in his career, not least to win 100 caps for Wales.

Alfie had it all, skill, pace and a fearless approach. He also captained Wales with a passion, having been a figure many didn't believe capable of doing the job.

Then there is Mark Jones, who was one of the most graceful runners we had in Wales.

He had blistering pace and his defence was underestimated.

But more than anything I admire his strength of character to come back from not one career threatening knee injury but two,

'I always found that players like the Tuilagi brothers, as good as they are at what they do, were easier to play against'

and all the while not losing any of his pace. Those guys never took anything for granted, and I have tried to adopt that approach.

Scott Johnson is someone who opened my eyes when he first came to work with the Wales team about six years ago.

I thought I was fairly near the finished article but he made me realise I could get so much better.

I needed to brush up on my skills and game-awareness and refine many points of my game that I believed were more or less okay.

It just goes to show that there is always room for improvement, always a need to work on the basics of the game like passing, kicking and tackling.

It's when you think you've made it that you get a kick up the backside in this game.

MY PHOTO ALBUM
Part 2

Shane tells us more stories behind the pictures from some memorable moments during his career, on and off the pitch

A kick ahead and the chase is on...

⊗ France try, part 1, March 2008

The start of my memorable try against France on the afternoon we won the Grand Slam again. I kicked the ball forward and then I needed the Gods to smile on me.

⊗ France try, part 2, March 2008

Bingo. The try is scored, it's midway through the second half, and we're on our way to glory.

...I get to the ball first and Wales are set for their second Grand Slam in four years

A jump for joy as Martyn Williams and Stephen Jones race to join in the celebrations

France try, part 3, March 2008

You can see what it means to me, Alun Wyn Jones, Martyn Williams and Stephen Jones.

Lap of honour after France match, 2008

Job done! The medal is around my neck, and all the pressure has lifted. We've beaten France to win the Grand Slam and walking around the pitch to thank the fans is just like being in heaven. To see the joy on people's faces...brilliant!

Job done and it's time to toast another Grand Slam

EDF Cup final success at Twickenham

EDF Energy Cup final, April 2008

Again, you can't buy moments like this, which came after we'd beaten Leicester in the EDF Energy Cup final at Twickenham in 2008. It's me with (from left to right) Huw Bennett, Ian Gough, Lee Byrne and Jonny Vaughton. What made that day all the more special was that the year before we had been hammered by the Tigers in the same game, when a calamitous first-half meant we were out of it by half-time. So this felt like payback – and any win at Twickenham is special.

Testimonial, 2008

Running out for my testimonial against Leicester in August 2008 at the Liberty Stadium. While it was a testimonial game it was also full-on as it was close to the start of the season and a chance for both teams to assess where they were. However, it was a privilege to have such a great team come to Swansea in my honour and having all my friends and family there to share it meant the world. We put in a good performance and there was a good crowd. I'll never forget that day.

What a day – my testimonial match

Belting out the national anthem, 2008

There is little to compare with the feeling you get at this moment. I always sing the anthem, but I don't belt it out like Alun Wyn Jones does (as you can see from this shot). He is the only person you can hear, but that takes nothing away from it! Being part of the anthem is one of things that makes me scared of retiring. I will miss it so much.

Land Of My Fathers rings out at the Millennium Stadium

Proud to wear another red shirt – this time for the British and Irish Lions

Lions' selection, 2009

This was taken on the day I learned of my selection for the Lions' 2009 tour to South Africa. Unlike in 2005 when we were told by text, we had to wait for the announcement to be made on Sky Sports. I was training at the Ospreys training ground in Llandarcy at the time and others told me I was in because they saw it before I did. A great feeling.

Time to go home lads...it's too cold!

Surfing, May 2009

This was a publicity stunt with me, Jamie Roberts, Lee Byrne, Tommy Bowe, Mike Phillips, Matthew Rees, Stephen Jones and Leigh Halfpenny before going to South Africa with the Lions in 2009, the shot taken on Caswell Bay near Mumbles on the western fringes of Swansea. Caswell is a great beach, but even though this was May it was a freezing cold day as you can see by the way we are wrapped up. No, we didn't actually go and do surfing in the sea – there was no way we were braving that! Am I a surfer? No. I had a go in Australia at the 2003 World Cup and spent most of the day just trying to stand up. I worry about sharks as well!

2008 trophies

2008 was some year. This was a chance for me to record it in the best way possible with all the trophies I'd won individually or as part of a team during that amazing 12 months.

Keeping me company here are (from left to right): the Triple Crown plate, the RBS Six Nations Player of the Championship gong, BBC Wales Sports Personality of the Year award, the RBS Six Nations trophy itself, the International Rugby Board Player of the Year trophy, the James Bevan Trophy (for beating Australia) and the EDF Energy Cup won with the Ospreys after we beat Leicester in the final at Twickenham.

A silver lining at
the end of 2008

'I'd like to think I'd have had the edge if me and the tortoise had raced'

▶ Tortoise versus the hare, 2009

Larking around at the team hotel in Cape Town on the 2009 Lions tour, Huw Evans, a photographer and great friend of all the players, persuaded me to pose for this unusual shot. It was a bit of a mickey-take because at the time there was footage of Bryan Habana racing a cheetah. All I was asked about on that trip was my potential duel with Habana.

I think originally they wanted me to race a sheep! I'd like to think I'd have had the edge if me and the tortoise had raced!

On your marks, get set, go...

A lonely feeling after a defeat at Croke Park

◀ Disappointment in Dublin, March 2010

You have to deal with losing in this job as well, and that's what I'm trying to do here as I contemplate 2010 Six Nations defeat to Ireland at Croke Park.

The crowd goes wild as a last-minute try wins the Wales-Scotland match in 2010

Winning try v Scotland,
February 2010

Going over for the try that clinched a dramatic late win for us against Scotland in the 2010 RBS Six Nations. Even though we were trailing for long spells I had a feeling we were going to come through. All I had to do was finish it off but it felt special. To this day I can't remember raising my arm in celebration before I touched the ball down. You fantasise about scoring the winning try in the 80th minute as a boy but few players actually experience doing it. Just look at the faces on the people in the crowd though. That's what makes this picture special for me.

Magners League win,
May 2010

This was after winning the Magners League Grand Final against Leinster at their home ground, the Royal Dublin Showground. They have a great record there, so to beat them and take a trophy home was special. Celebrating with your team-mates – Alun Wyn Jones and Nikki Walker here – like this is why you play the game.

Some unorthodox headwear after winning the Magners League in 2010

Tiger Woods watches a tee-shot during the 2010 Ryder Cup at Celtic Manor

AWAY FROM THE GAME

When he's not playing or training, Shane likes nothing better than relaxing with his family, an occasional round of golf and laughing at Homer Simpson

Away from rugby I love socialising with my mates whether it's meeting at the club and talking about old times or whatever.

I thrive on that sort of company because my friends know that when we meet up the last thing I want to talk about is rugby.

Usually we'll chat for five minutes initially and then we'll draw a line under it and talk about any old nonsense and have a good laugh.

And believe me, I get the mickey taken out of me as much as anyone.

I like doing things that I suppose a lot of others enjoy. I love playing golf, though I haven't played much in the recent past due to various injuries.

Tiger Woods is one of my sporting heroes, though he didn't have a great year last year!

I know how difficult golf is to master and for Tiger to have made it look so easy over the toughest courses in the world for so many years makes him a bit of a legend in my book.

But these days, much of my time is spent with my two young kids, Georgie and Carter; I love mucking about with them.

I'll pick them up from school and we'll have a couple of hours of just having a laugh really.

They keep me occupied to the point where I barely can

think about doing other things sometimes, but I wouldn't have it any other way.

It's difficult to do too much when you're a parent.

Unfortunately, me and Gail aren't very good cooks (I'm not sure she'll appreciate that!).

Cradling daughter Georgie before a testimonial match

WRU

Favourite show:
The Simpsons

The Foo Fighters, seen here performing at the Millennium Stadium in 2005, are a favourite of Shane's

Not to be confused with Jamie Oliver

'Anything with Jim Carrey will keep me transfixed. He's an acquired taste but I love the bloke'

We do eat well, we get through a lot of salads and I get through a lot of chicken and turkey.

My gran used to say that I ate so much turkey that I'd end up looking like one!

When I was a kid, with my parents being divorced, I used to have three Christmas dinners, one with my mam, one with dad and one with my grandparents.

When it comes to food though, I'm the type who doesn't tend to venture too far outside what I know I like, I'd never try to cook anything spectacular and Gail is the same.

It's the same with the kids who usually settle for oven chips or chicken dinosaurs.

I wish I could say I was Jamie Oliver but I'm not, though that's not to say I eat junk.

However, there is a special cupboard in our kitchen above the sink that contains all the sweets and chocolates that we have in the house. It kills me every time I open the door because I see them all knowing that I'm not allowed to have any.

How do I spend time when I'm not playing rugby and not running around after the kids? Well, I'll watch a bit of television, The Simpsons being my favourite show. I like the unreality of it all and I end up imagining what it would be like to live in a cartoon world. You know, I don't feel I'm that dissimilar sometimes to Homer Simpson!

If I'm going to watch a film, then anything with Jim Carrey in it will keep me transfixed. He's an acquired taste for most people, but I love the bloke. Ace Ventura: Pet Detective is my favourite watch.

When it comes to music, my preferences are fairly wide-ranging; I like a bit of everything and am not massively into any one group, though I do like the Foo Fighters.

I'm a pretty easy-going character away from rugby. I approach life positively and try to have time for as many people as possible. I try to be helpful, always, and I appreciate the same qualities in others.

I hate liars, whether they be tellers of white lies or big horrible black ones, it's just a trait that really annoys me.

And I can't stand people who are tight, people who forget to pay you back money you have lent them but who then insist you pay them the next day if it's the other way around.

But I find it easy to get on with people by just being myself. My valley is a safe haven for me, everyone knows me and treats me the same as anyone else – and I wouldn't want it any other way.

I like nothing better than on a spare Saturday wandering down to the park and watching my brother play for Amman United and having a chat with the regulars on the touchline.

I also work with the youth down there and that's something I get a real kick out of as well.

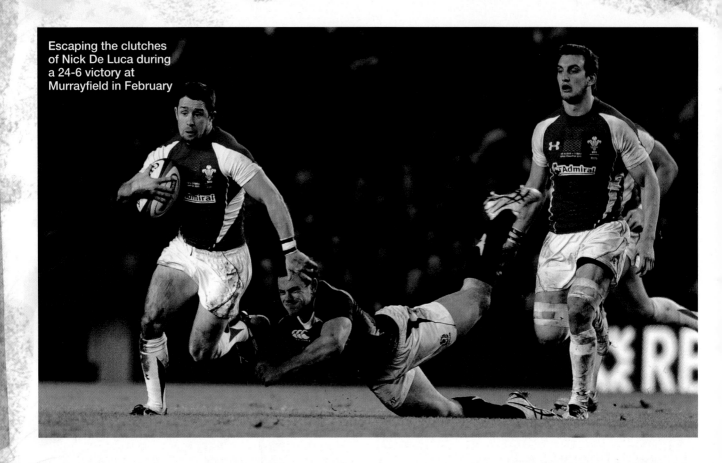

Escaping the clutches of Nick De Luca during a 24-6 victory at Murrayfield in February

HANGING UP MY BOOTS

It is generally anticipated that Shane will wear the Wales jersey for the final time during this year's World Cup but his future plans haven't been finalised

Everyone seems to have assumed that I'm retiring from international rugby for definite after the World Cup.

Not quite accurate.

What I've said is that it would be the logical time to go, the truth is I have not categorically committed to it. And let me tell you when I do have to go I will be devastated.

That said, I am fully aware that at 34 years of age, I am in the twilight of my Test career. Someone who plays on the wing is reliant on speed, agility and quick reactions, all the things that tend to wane with advancing years.

Look in the record books. There can't be too many wingers who have gone on past their mid-30s at the very highest level, or even reached that age still cutting it in the highest company.

I would hate to hang on past my sell-by date and end up being unceremoniously dropped from the Wales squad, being told I was no longer good enough in the process. That would kill me.

So I want to go on my own terms. I want to know myself when the time is right, and I believe that I will.

When the World Cup is over, it will realistically be time for the younger guys to come through, but if I'm still feeling the way I do now, sharp, eager, hungry and happy with my form, then...

Look, you never say never. Perhaps the time will be right for me then, though I want to go on playing at regional

level for another two years. That for me is an honest appraisal of what I have left in me.

After that, it will be time to hang up the boots, professionally that is, because I can still see me playing for my village side on a Saturday afternoon, which as far

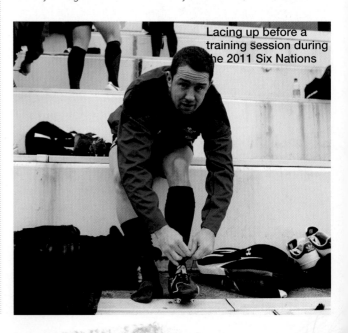

Lacing up before a training session during the 2011 Six Nations

'I have always enjoyed meeting people, ever since I used to work in the Job Centre'

as I'm concerned is the time for playing rugby. What else will I do? Well, that's something I've been thinking about quite a bit lately.

I have my own promotions business and some property, but there are other things I'd like to try my hand at in the future.

With that in mind I've been working for two businesses, Oil4Wales, which is a domestic heating oil supplier run by a friend of mine, Colin Owens, and 24/7 Heating Care, a company owned by my father-in-law.

I've got involved on the promotions and customer care sides of these businesses and I'm doing it because I want to learn new skills and be ready to have something to offer the real world when I can't play rugby anymore.

If rugby was all I thought about these days I'd go completely around the bend, you have to have a different focus.

I've invested a bit with these two companies and I've been getting out and about and meeting people.

The aim is to give a bit of a personal touch and we've found that me meeting them has made a difference.

I have always enjoyed meeting people, ever since I used to work in the Job Centre before I became a rugby player.

I've often wondered how far I could have gone in the employment service if I had stayed there because the people I worked with said I was good at what I did.

But I guess I'll never know now, and I can't say I'd swap what I've done in rugby to find out!

The property thing is another area that I can see myself doing more in.

I've gone into business with Ryan Jones where we own a buy-to-let company and that is doing well.

We've not much time to devote to it at the moment, others do the donkey work, but we've both invested some money in it and it is something that we can give more attention to when we have stopped playing.

I enjoy the world of business, and I hope there will be more opportunities for me when I stop playing.

I would also like to do media work because I think it's a great way of staying in touch with the top level of the game.

I've always welcomed dealing with the press, I've always tried to be myself in any interviews I've done and I'd like to think journalists have appreciated that.

But when I'm no longer playing I just hope that people remember me as someone who gave his 100 per cent all every time he played.

No matter what you do in the game, the tries, the records, the trophies, the awards, you can't be all things to all people. There are always going to be some who don't really care for what you do.

But I'd like even them to recognise that I always gave my all. That's the best legacy I could leave.

Shane has gone into business with Ryan Jones, seen here giving an inspirational team-talk at Croke Park in 2008

'I'm just an ordinary lad from the Amman Valley who has been able to fulfill his dream'

SEE THE BEST RUGBY UNDER THE SUN

130TH ANNIVERSARY CELEBRATION GAME

Wales v Barbarians
4 June 2011

Wales v England
13 August 2011

Wales v Argentina
20 August 2011

Get your tickets now
Prices start at £15 – Family tickets available
Call **08442 777 888** or visit **wru.co.uk/tickets**
or contact your local rugby club for information

'I hope you enjoy this souvenir magazine as much as I have enjoyed putting it all together'

Shane Williams has lit up Welsh rugby for over a decade and is one of the sport's great entertainers. Since making his debut for his country as a fresh-faced youngster in 2000, he has scored 55 international tries – second only to David Campese among top-level players. His pace, agility and breathtaking side-steps have run opposition defences ragged the world over.

In this official WRU souvenir magazine, Shane looks back on his glittering career, as well as describing his upbringing, the struggle he faced to establish himself in the Wales squad and what it means to wear the red jersey. He chooses his favourite games, top 10 tries and provides a unique insight into the men he has played alongside and against.

There is a special section on the Grand Slams of 2005 and 2008, plus a flick through his photo album with the story behind the pictures told by the man himself. With the World Cup in New Zealand, starting in September, potentially providing his international swansong, this special publication pays tribute to one of the all-time greats.

£3.99

ISBN 978-1-906802-64-6

9 781906 802646